Second Edition

HOW TO . . . CONVERT THE METRIC SYSTEM INTO THE U.S. SYSTEM AND VICE VERSA

Written and Compiled by:

CHRISTINE N. GOVONI VOGEL

ADAMS PRESS
CHICAGO, ILLINOIS

International Standard Book Number:
ISBN 0-9600656-0-1

First Edition, April 15, 1972

Second Edition, 1973

International Standard Book Number: ISBN 0-9600656-0-1

Library of Congress Registration Number A. 329338 Class "A"

A word of caution: Use of this book is at the user's risk, and no warranty is made, also for mis-interpretations and/or mis-calculations. Check and re-check in the same manner as translating a foreign language.

Suitable communications will always be gratefully received and acknowledged.

C. N. VOGEL, P.O. Box 103, Bellevue, Washington, 98009, U.S.A.

Price, $3.95 Per Copy

Printed at Adams Press, Chicago, Illinois U.S.A.

To my devoted husband, Richard,
without whose love and understanding
this book would never have come into
existence.

Christine N. Govoni Vogel

AUTHOR'S BIOGRAPHY

PROFESSION

School Guidance Counselor, Educator and Lecturer.

Born in Roanoke, Virginia;

Daughter of Colonel (ret.) Joseph Francis and Mary E. (Lawson) Govoni.

MARRIED

Richard P. Vogel, July 28, 1966 in Coeur d'Alene, Idaho.

EDUCATION

Attended the Polytechnical High School, Riverside, California, 1950.

Attended the University of Alaska, 1950 - 52.

Received a Bachelor of Science degree in Education from the Concord College in Athens, West Virginia in 1955.

Received a Masters degree in Education from the University of Maryland in 1963.

Postgraduate courses at other Colleges.

APPOINTMENTS HELD

Junior High School Teacher, Hampton, Virginia, 1955.

Teacher, grades seven to twelve, Kinjo Gakuin School, Nagoya, Japan, 1955 - 56.

Core Teacher, Catonsville, Maryland, 1956 - 60.

Teacher of Interior Decoration, Adult Evening Classes, Catonsville, Maryland, 1964 - 66.

School Guidance Counselor, Baltimore County Schools,

Catonsville, Maryland, 1960 - 67.

School Guidance Counselor, Bellevue Junior High School, Bellevue, Washington, since 1967.

Volunteer Counselor for the King County Community Services, State of Washington, since 1972.

PROFESSIONAL AFFILIATIONS

National Education Association (NEA)

American Personnel and Guidance Association (APGA)

American School Counselor Association (ASCA)

Washington Education Association (WEA)

Bellevue Education Association (BEA)

Bellevue School Counselors Association (BSCA Secretary-Treasurer)

Bellevue Parent Teacher Student Association (PTSA)

OTHER MEMBERSHIPS

Alpha Sigma Alpha (Chaplain)

Kappa Omicron Phi (President, Senior of the Year)

Phi Delta Gamma; Upsilon Chapter (Charter member and Secretary for two years)

Alaska Alumni Association (Charter member of the Washington State Chapter)

HONORS

May Court, Attendant to May Queen, Concord College 1954.

Awarded a General Electric Graduate Fellowship at the Syracuse University, New York, 1961.

LISTED IN

"Who's Who of American Women"

"Dictionary of International Biography"

"The National Register of Prominent
Americans and International Notables"

"Two Thousand Women of Achievement"

"The World Who's Who of Women"

"International Who's Who in Community Service"

ACKNOWLEDGEMENTS

In this "Second Edition" of my book: HOW TO CONVERT THE
METRIC SYSTEM INTO THE U.S. SYSTEM AND VICE VERSA, I would
like to compliment and thank with my utmost respect and
appreciation:

The Honorable Senator Claiborne Pell (D) Rhode Island
and the Honorable Senator Daniel K. Inouye (D) Hawaii for
introducing A BILL which was read twice and referred to the
Committee on Commerce on August 16, 1972. It was reported
by the Honorable Senator Warren G. Magnuson (D) Washington,
Chairman.

Calendar No. 1018, 92D CONGRESS, 2D SESSION, S.2483.

(Report No. 92-1067)

A BILL

To provide a national program in order to make
the international metric system the official
and standard system of measurement in the
United States and to provide for converting
to the general use of such system within ten
years after the date of enactment of this Act.

I received a copy of "The Metric Conversion Act" as it
passed the Senate and a copy of "The Committee Report" (by
mail) from the Honorable Senator Claiborne Pell (D) Rhode
Island. From the Honorable Senator Warren G. Magnuson (D)

Washington, Chairman of the Committee, I received a copy of his book: <u>THE DARK SIDE OF THE MARKETPLACE.</u> I found it to be not only interesting but useful and up to date.

The Honorable Secretary of Commerce, Mr. Peter G. Peterson, recommended sending a copy of my book to Mr. L. E. Barbrow, Coordinator of Metric Activities, National Bureau of Standards, Washington, D.C.

Mr. Barbrow and his colleague, Mr. J. V. Odom, reviewed, corrected and offered some suggestions for the "Second Edition". Their helpful statements were accompanied by several government publications. These publications were useful guidelines as I revised and compiled this "Second Edition", making it a more accurate "Guide and Reference Book".

I can not end these acknowledgements with just a "Thank you". I feel that the readers and users of this book should be aware of the sincere efforts of the above mentioned dignitaries. It has been my experience that our elected and appointed officials in the various branches of the United States Government are working with and serving all the people of our GREAT NATION. May their tireless efforts continue for the benefit of all mankind!

<u>These acknowledgements are expressions of my own feelings, and none of the men mentioned should be held accountable for the contents of this book.</u>

PREFACE

Professionals in the fields of science, medicine, government
and industry are already performing some of their daily
tasks by computing with the less complicated but more simplified, time saving and accurate system of weights and measurements called the "Metric System".

Today's youth are anxious and eager to acquire knowledge in
all areas of science, current world and national affairs.
With the increasing demands in the U.S. for short - cuts in
learning, many valuable hours could be gained by adopting
the decimal based "Metric System".

Our population is composed of almost every race and nation
on earth and certainly every man, women and child faces,
at one time or another, the problem of converting meter,
gram, liter, carat, grain, stere, etc. into ounce, yard,
gallon, mile, etc.

"Why not one system" is mostly the helpseeking cry when he
or she is trembling with anger, while concluding that a
parallel between the two systems just does not exist.

However, to compute metric values is a procedure simular to
the U.S. monetary system. Metric denominations are written
as decimals, a system of reckoning by tens or tenths.

For some years, I have toyed with the idea of compiling my
knowledge of the "Metric System" into book form.

Information for this book was obtained through informal

research and personal experience while purchasing imported
goods and traveling abroad.

Therefore, it is my logical wish and conclusion that others
who must deal with both systems of measurement will find
this book not only an easy to comprehend reference but also
a valuable addition to any private or public library.

According to statistics, 92% of the world's population are
using the "Metric System".

On August 18, 1972 the United States Senate overwhelmingly
approved by voice vote and without opposition the conversion
of the United States to the "Metric System".

This question with so many pro's and con's was pending and
from time to time debated on since the turn of this century.

The decision to adopt or not to adopt the "Metric System" in
the United States was still pending when the "First Edition"
of this book was already in print and being used by people
in all walks of life; including Universities, Technical
Institutes and Governmental Agencies - from coast to coast.

May the following chapters be of assistance as a helpful
"Guide and Reference" towards a better understanding and an
easier and more accurate use of both systems.

                                        Christine N. Govoni Vogel

Bellevue, Washington

THE METRIC SYSTEM IN THE PAST AND PRESENT

The establishment of a device and formulas to measure and calculate distances with more exactness was seemingly the most troublesome question to be solved during the late years of the seventeenth century.

Delambre and Méchain, the two French academicians, made it their project to find a method which should be accurate enough to measure length, weight, volume and other physical compound units with the utmost exactness and with the characteristic of being memorized instantly.

Negotiations between the National Assembly of France and the Academy of Science of Paris consumed costly time between the years of 1790 and 1792.

To begin with, the meridian arc between the northern French City of Dunkirk and the Spanish City of Barcelona had to be measured.

This project lasted, according to the historians, another seven years. By 1799 they calculated the newly established meridian quadrant and adopted the ten millionth part of it as an established unit to measure the distance between two points. Soon after the new unit had been established, the new system developed unforeseen conveniences.

Finding new formulas to calculate length, weight and volume was only a matter of a comparatively short time.

The newly established method became legalized in France by a decree of law in the year of 1801.

New names had to be found to describe the multitude of new
units and prefixes and to make them sound right, also
understandable in the everyday common language.
Greek and Latin, the languages of ancient history and old
sciences, provided the convenient vocabulary.
The Greek Word "metron" became the French Word "mètre"
meaning length.
The Greek Word "deka" became the French Word "deca" meaning
ten of any unit. The Greek Word "hekaton" became the French
Word "hecto" meaning hundred of any unit. The Greek Word
"khilioi" became the French Word "kilo" meaning thousand of
any unit. The Greek Word "murias" became the French Word
"myria" meaning ten thousand of any unit. The Greek Word
"stereos" became the French Word "stere" meaning a solid
unit mostly wood, timber etc. The Greek Word "litron"
became the French Word "litre" meaning a liquid measure.
The Greek Word "gramma" became the French Word "gram"
meaning a small unit of weight.
The Latin Word "area" became the French Word "are" for land
surfaces. The Latin Word "decem" became the French Word
"deci" meaning tenth of ..... . The Latin Word "centum"
became the French Word "centi" meaning hundredth of ..... .
The Latin Word "mille" became the French Word "milli"
meaning thousandth of ..... .
On January 11, 1840, French Laws made the "Metric System"
obligatory throughout France.

Germany, its closest neighbor, began its movement toward
adoption of the new method in 1860 and by 1868, it became
optional there to use the new standards, but on January 1,
1872, an act of law made the metric system compulsory.

Other countries have yielded to the example of these two
industrious Western European Nations and since then the
metric system has replaced old and long outdated methods
throughout the world. The United States of America did not
adopt the metric system. However, Congress authorized its
use within the United States but did not make it compulsory.

Ever since, intense movements have met with very strong
opposition before and after the turn of this century, while
trying to adopt the universal system as the only legal unit
for weights and measurements in this country.

Inconveniences and anticipated confusion during the
transition stage were the strongest points for not accepting
the metric units as obligatory.

Progress means improving or sometimes the destruction of old
methods, and such steps are always costly and connected with
difficulties.

The "seven base units" for the "International System" (SI):

commonly known as the "METRIC SYSTEM".

Length = meter (symbol: m)

Mass = kilogram (symbol: kg)

Time = second (symbol: s)

Electric current = ampere (symbol: A)

Thermodynamic temperature = Kelvin (symbol: K)

Amount of Substance = mole (symbol: mol)

Light intensity = candela (symbol: cd)

The "supplementary units".

Plane angle, unit: radian; symbol: rad

Solid angle, unit: steradian; symbol: sr

The "derived units".

Area, unit: square meter; symbol: m^2

Volume, unit: cubic meter; symbol: m^3

Frequency, unit: hertz; symbol: Hz; derivation: s^{-1}

Density, unit: kilogram per cubic meter; symbol: kg/m^3

Velocity, unit: meter per second; symbol: m/s

Angular velocity, unit: radian per second; symbol: rad/s

Acceleration, unit: meter per second squared; symbol: m/s^2

Angular acceleration, unit: radian per second squared;

symbol: rad/s^2

Force, unit: newton; symbol: N; derivation: $(kg \cdot m/s^2)$

Pressure, unit: pascal (Pa) or: newton per square meter;

symbol: N/m^2

Kinematic viscosity, unit: square meter per second;

symbol: m^2/s

Dynamic viscosity, unit: newton-second per square meter;

symbol: $N \cdot s/m^2$

Work, energy, quantity of heat, unit: joule; symbol: J

derivation: $(N \cdot m)$

Power, unit: watt; symbol: W; derivation: (J/s)

Electric charge, unit: coulomb; symbol: C

derivation: $(A \cdot s)$

Voltage, potential difference, electromotive force,

unit: volt; symbol: V; derivation: (W/A)

Electric field strength, unit: volt per meter; symbol: V/m

Electric resistance, unit: ohm, symbol: Ω; derivation: (V/A)

Electric capacitance, unit: farad; symbol: F; deriv.: $(A \cdot s/V)$

Magnetic flux, unit: weber; symbol: Wb; deriv.: $(V \cdot s)$

Inductance, unit: henry; symbol: H; derivation: $(V \cdot s/A)$

Magnetic flux density, unit: tesla; symbol: T; deriv.: (Wb/m^2)

Magnetic field strength, unit: ampere per meter; symbol: A/m

Magnetomotive force, unit: ampere; symbol: A

Flux of light; unit: lumen; symbol: lm; deriv.: $(cd \cdot sr)$

Luminance, unit: candela per square meter; symbol: cd/m^2

Illumination, unit: lux; symbol: lx; derivation: (lm/m^2)

THE FOLLOWING PREFIXES MAY BE APPLIED TO ALL METRIC UNITS.

Names of "multiples" and "sub-multiples" of the units are formed by means of the following prefixes:

"Multiples" and "Sub-multiples"	Prefixes	Symbols
$1\ 000\ 000\ 000\ 000 = 10^{12}$	tera	T
$1\ 000\ 000\ 000 = 10^{9}$	giga	G
$1\ 000\ 000 = 10^{6}$	mega	M
$1\ 000 = 10^{3}$	kilo	k
$100 = 10^{2}$	hecto	h
$10 = 10^{1}$	deka	da
$0.1 = 10^{-1}$	deci	d
$0.01 = 10^{-2}$	centi	c
$0.001 = 10^{-3}$	milli	m
$0.000\ 001 = 10^{-6}$	micro	μ
$0.000\ 000\ 001 = 10^{-9}$	nano	n
$0.000\ 000\ 000\ 001 = 10^{-12}$	pico	p
$0.000\ 000\ 000\ 000\ 001 = 10^{-15}$	femto	f
$0.000\ 000\ 000\ 000\ 000\ 001 = 10^{-18}$	atto	a

MEASURES OF LENGTH.

The "meter" as the principal and basic unit bears the same
name as the measuring instrument which is used to determine
the distance between two given or hitherto un-established
points.
A "meter" is a unit of length equal to: 1 650 763.73 wave-
lengths in a vacuum of the orange-red radiation of Krypton 86.
The length of "one meter" is often but nevertheless erro-
neously assumed to be equal to the length of the United
States physical measurement unit of "one yard" (or assumed
that one meter is three feet plus three inches in length).

Unit = 1 meter in length.

Sub-multiples:

     Sub-multiple = decimeter (10 to one meter)

     Sub-multiple = centimeter (100 to one meter)

     Sub-multiple = millimeter (1 000 to one meter)

Special sub-multiples:

     angstrom, nanometer, micrometer, picometer, etc.

     are not generally used in the SI .

     For exact definitions see page 8

Multiples:

     Multiple = dekameter (10 meters in length)

     Multiple = hectometer (100 meters in length)

     Multiple = kilometer (1 000 meters in length)

As a "decimal" system, metric numbers multiply and divide
equal and efficently with the decimal point.

The METRIC decimal system avoids completely the time consuming
balancing of compound numbers, and therefore has won its
worldwide popularity and acceptance because of its systematic
simplicity. By the written and verbal expressing of a number
which is composed of meter(s), decimeter(s), centimeter(s),
and millimeter(s) as decimals, the decimeter(s) signify always
as tenths, the centimeter(s) as hundredths, and the milli-
meter(s) as thousandths, behind the decimal point.

FOR EXAMPLE:

If the measured distance between two points is 3 meters,
1 decimeter, 4 centimeters and 8 millimeters; it would be
written as 3.148 meters or it could be written as 31.48 decimeters, 314.8 centimeters, or 3148 millimeters but 3.148 meters
is the customary expression.

Measuring larger distances:

For measuring distances between cities, towns, countries and
continents, (etc.) the multiple term "kilometer" is used as
a basic unit for the general terms. The multiple designations
"dekameter", and "hectometer", are technical terms used
mainly for land measurement and for surveying purposes.

FOR EXAMPLE:

If the distance between city "A" to city "B" is measured as

being 220 kilometers and 685 meters, it would normally be
written as 220.685 kilometers. This is the simplified
expression. However; "rounded off" 221 km is correct.
No one would write: 220 kilometers, 6 hectometers, 8 deca-
meters, and 5 meters.

Converting:

To obtain quantity in "U.S. units" from that in "Metric units"
or vice versa multiply by appropriate conversion factor.

For example:

"Metric" to "U.S."

How many meters are in 120 yards?

  1 yard = 0.914 4 meters

120 yards = 0.914 4 times 120 = 109.728 meters

(109.73 meters rounded off).

"U.S." to "Metric".

How many yards are in 30 meters?

  1 meter = 1.093 613 yards

30 times 1.093 613 yards = 32.808 39 yards

(32.81 yards rounded off).

The following pages provide the reader with ready to use
converted columns, "Metric" to "U.S." and "U.S." to "Metric".
Also columns are provided with related denominations.
The sequences from 1 to 10 of the particular units are
easy to convert.

For example:

How many inches are contained in 15 centimeters?

```
        10 cm = 3.937 10 in
plus      5 cm = 1.968 55 in
Total:   15 cm = 5.905 65 in    or: "rounded off": 6 inches
One may compute: 1 cm = 0.393 71 in times 15 = 5.905 65 in
            or: 5 cm = 1.968 55 in times  3 = 5.905 65 in
The result will be the same, likened to: 2 times 4 = 8
                                     or: 8 times 1 = 8
                                     or: 4 times 2 = 8
```

The decimals can be increased or decreased by a relatively small amount for the sake of convenience or commonly known as "rounding off". For "commonly" non-technical conversion's see tables on page 154 - 155

Note: Only technical persons in technical usage would use such exact conversions.

Note: Throughout this book some units are denoted as

"obsolete",

which means that these units are no longer "official" units within the "METRIC SYSTEM" or the "U.S. SYSTEM". However; recipies, formulas and some books from "metric" countries may still use these "obsolete" terms.

Sometimes we encounter such units or "obsolete" "weights and measures".

BUT: DO NOT USE "OBSOLETE" UNITS!
====================================

METER.

(Basic Unit of the Metric System).

Sub-multiples:

    decimeter(s)   centimeter(s)   millimeter(s)

Multiples:

    dekameter(s)   hectometer(s)   kilometer(s)

"One meter" in length is equal to:

10 decimeters   100 centimeters   1 000 millimeters

"One meter" as a "fraction" in the "meter's multiple(s) is:

1/10 dekameter   1/100 hectometer   1/1000 kilometer

How to denote "meter's" as "metric sub-multiples":

m	dm	cm	mm
1	10	100	1 000
2	20	200	2 000
3	30	300	3 000
4	40	400	4 000
5	50	500	5 000
6	60	600	6 000
7	70	700	7 000
8	80	800	8 000
9	90	900	9 000
10	100	1 000	10 000

How to denote "meter(s)" as "metric multiples".

m	dam	hm	km
1	0.1	0.01	0.001
2	0.2	0.02	0.002
3	0.3	0.03	0.003
4	0.4	0.04	0.004
5	0.5	0.05	0.005
6	0.6	0.06	0.006
7	0.7	0.07	0.007
8	0.8	0.08	0.008
9	0.9	0.09	0.009
10	1.0	0.10	0.010

Converting "metric measures" to "U.S. measures":

"One meter" in length is equal to::

39.370 08 inches,   4.970 97 links,   3.280 840 feet,

1.093 613 yards   0.198 839 rods,   0.049 71 chains,

0.000 621 37 miles.

How to denote "meter(s)" in length as "U.S. measurements":

m	in	link	ft	yd
1	39.370 08	4.970 97	3.280 840	1.093 613
2	78.740 16	9.941 94	6.561 680	2.187 226
3	118.110 24	14.912 91	9.842 520	3.280 839
4	157.480 32	19.883 88	13.123 360	4.374 452
5	196.850 40	24.854 85	16.402 400	5.468 065

m	in	link	ft	yd
6	236.220 48	29.825 82	19.685 040	6.561 678
7	275.590 56	34.796 79	22.965 880	7.655 291
8	314.960 64	39.767 76	26.246 720	8.748 904
9	354.330 72	44.738 73	29.527 560	9.842 517
10	393.700 80	49.709 70	32.808 400	10.936 130

How to denote "meter(s)" in length as "U.S. measurements":

m	rod	ch	mi
1	0.198 839	0.049 71	0.000 621 37
2	0.397 678	0.099 42	0.001 242 74
3	0.596 517	0.149 13	0.001 864 11
4	0.795 356	0.198 84	0.002 485 48
5	0.994 195	0.248 55	0.003 106 85
6	1.193 034	0.298 26	0.003 728 22
7	1.391 873	0.347 97	0.004 349 59
8	1.590 712	0.397 68	0.004 970 96
9	1.789 551	0.447 39	0.005 592 33
10	1.988 390	0.497 10	0.006 213 70

DECIMETER.

("Sub-multiple" of the "meter").

Sub-multiple:

   centimeter   millimeter

"One decimeter" in length is equal to:

10 centimeters   100 millimeters

"One decimeter" as a "decimal" is:

0.1 meter

How to denote "decimeter(s)" as "U.S. measurements":

"One decimeter" in length is equal to:

3.937 008 0 in   0.328 084 0 ft   0.109 361 3 yd

CENTIMETER.

("Sub-multiple" of the "meter").

Sub-multiple:

   millimeter

"One centimeter" in length is equal to:

   10 millimeters

"One centimeter" as a "decimal" is:

   0.1 decimeter   0.01 meter

"One centimeter" as a "fraction" is:

   1/10 decimeter   1/100 meter

       Converting "centimeter(s)" to "U.S. measures":

"One centimeter = 0.393 700 8 in or slightly more than 3/8 in

0.049 710 link   0.032 808 40 ft   0.010 936 13 yd

0.001 988 rod   0.000 497 0 ch   0.000 006 mi

How to denote "centimeter(s)" as "metric multiples":

cm	dm	m	dam	hm	km
1	0.1	0.01	0.001	0.000 1	0.000 01
2	0.2	0.02	0.002	0.000 2	0.000 02
3	0.3	0.03	0.003	0.000 3	0.000 03
4	0.4	0.04	0.004	0.000 4	0.000 04
5	0.5	0.05	0.005	0.000 5	0.000 05
6	0.6	0.06	0.006	0.000 6	0.000 06
7	0.7	0.07	0.007	0.000 7	0.000 07
8	0.8	0.08	0.008	0.000 8	0.000 08
9	0.9	0.09	0.009	0.000 9	0.000 09
10	1.0	0.10	0.010	0.001 0	0.000 10

How to denote "centimeter(s)" as "U.S. measurements":

cm	in	link	ft	yd
1	0.393 700 8	0.049 710	0.032 808 40	0.010 936 13
2	0.787 401 6	0.099 420	0.065 616 80	0.021 872 26
3	1.181 102 4	0.149 130	0.098 425 20	0.032 808 39
4	1.574 803 2	0.198 840	0.131 233 60	0.043 744 52
5	1.968 504 0	0.248 550	0.164 042 00	0.054 680 65
6	2.362 204 8	0.298 260	0.196 850 40	0.065 616 78
7	2.755 905 6	0.347 970	0.229 658 80	0.076 552 91
8	3.149 606 4	0.397 680	0.262 467 20	0.087 489 04
9	3.543 307 2	0.447 390	0.295 275 60	0.098 425 17
10	3.937 008 0	0.497 100	0.328 084 00	0.109 361 30

How to denote "centimeter(s)" as "U.S. measurements":

cm	rod	ch	mi
1	0.001 988	0.000 497 0	0.000 006 0
2	0.003 976	0.000 994 0	0.000 012 0
3	0.005 964	0.001 491 0	0.000 018 0
4	0.007 952	0.001 988 0	0.000 024 0
5	0.008 940	0.002 485 0	0.000 030 0
6	0.011 928	0.002 982 0	0.000 036 0
7	0.013 916	0.003 479 0	0.000 042 0
8	0.015 904	0.003 776 0	0.000 048 0
9	0.017 892	0.004 473 0	0.000 054 0
10	0.019 880	0.004 970 0	0.000 060 0

MILLIMETER.

("Sub-multiple" of the "meter").

"One millimeter" as a metric "decimal" is:

   0.1 centimeter   0.01 decimeter   0.001 meter

"One millimeter" as a "metric fraction" is:

   1/10 centimeter   1/100 decimeter   1/1 000 meter

How to denote "millimeter" as the "U.S. measurement":"inch".

     1 mm is 0.039 370 078 07 in (exactly)

     1 mm is 0.039 370 079 in (rounded off)

     1 mm is 0.039 370 08 in (rounded off)

     1 mm is 0.039 370 1 in (rounded off)

     1 mm is 0.039 370 in (rounded off)

     1 mm is 0.039 37 in (rounded off)

     1 mm is 0.039 4 in (rounded off)

     1 mm is 0.04 in (rounded off)

How to denote "millimeter(s)" as "metric decimals":

mm	cm	dm	m
1	0.1	0.01	0.001
2	0.2	0.02	0.002
3	0.3	0.03	0.003
4	0.4	0.04	0.004
5	0.5	0.05	0.005
6	0.6	0.06	0.006
7	0.7	0.07	0.007
8	0.8	0.08	0.008
9	0.9	0.09	0.009
10	1.0	0.10	0.010

DEKAMETER.

("Multiple" of the "meter").

"Sub-multiples":

    meters   decimeters   centimeters   millimeters

"Multiples":

    hectometer(s)   kilometer(s)

"One dekameter" in length is equal to:

    10 meters   100 decimeters   1 000 centimeters

    10 000 millimeters

"One dekameter" as a "decimal" in the "dekameter's multiples" is:

    0.1 hectometer   0.010 kilometer

"One dekameter" as a "fraction" in the "dekameter's multiples" is:

    1/10 hectometer   1/100 kilometer

    How to denote "dekameter" as "U.S. measures":

"One dekameter" in length is equal to:

393.700 8 inches	49.709 7 links	32.808 40 feet
10.936 13 yd	1.988 39 rod	0.497 1 chain
0.006 213 8 mile		

HECTOMETER.

("Multiple" of the "meter").

"Sub-multiples":

    dekameters   meters   decimeters

    centimeters   millimeters

"Multiples":

    kilometer(s)

"One hectometer" in length is equal to:

   10 dekameters   100 meters   1 000 decimeters

   100 000 millimeters

"One hectometer" as a "decimal" in the "hectometer's

multiple(s)" is:

   0.1 kilometer

"One hectometer" as a "fraction" in the "hectometer's

multiple(s)" is:

   1/10 kilometer

      How to denote "hectometer" as "U.S. measures":

"One hectometer" in length is equal to:

3 937 08 inches	497.097 links	328.084 0 feet
109.361 3 yards	19.883 9 rods	4.971 0 chains
0.062 138 mile		

KILOMETER.

("Multiple" of the "meter").

"Sub-multiples"

hectometers	dekameters	meters
decimeters	centimeters	millimeters

"One kilometer" in length is equal to:

10 hectometers	100 dekameters	1 000 meters
10 000 decimeters	100 000 centimeters	
1 000 000 millimeters		

How to denote "kilometer" as "U.S. measures":

"One kilometer" in length is equal to:

39 371 inches	4 970.97 links	3 280.84 feet
1 093.613 yards	198.839 rods	49.71 chains
0.621 37 mile		

YARD.

"Sub-multiples":

inch(es)	link(s)	foot; feet

"Multiples":

rod(s)	chain(s)	mile(s)

"One yard" in length is equal to:

36 inches	4.545 45 links	3 feet
0.181 818 rod	0.045 454 5 chain	
0.000 568 18 mile		

How to denote "yard" as "metric measures":

"One yard" in length is equal to:

0.9144 meter	9.144 decimeters
91.44 centimeters	0.091 44 dekameter
0.009 144 hectometer	0.000 914 4 kilometer

How to denote "yard(s)" as "metric decimals":

yd	m	dm	cm	mm
1	0.914 4	9.144	91.44	914.4
2	1.828 8	18.288	182.88	1 828.8
3	2.743 2	27.432	274.32	2 743.2
4	3.657 6	36.576	365.76	3 657.6
5	4.572 0	45.720	457.20	4 572.0
6	5.486 4	54.864	548.64	5 486.4
7	6.400 8	64.008	640.08	6 400.8
8	7.315 2	73.152	731.52	7 315.2
9	8.229 6	82.296	822.96	8 229.6
10	9.144 0	91.440	914.40	9 144.0

How to denote "yard(s)" as other "U.S. measures:

yd	in	link	ft	rod	ch	mi
1	36	4.545 45	3	0.181 818	0.045 455	0.000 568
2	72	9.090 90	6	0.363 636	0.090 910	0.001 136
3	108	13.636 35	9	0.545 454	0.136 365	0.001 704
4	144	18.181 80	12	0.727 272	0.181 820	0.002 272
5	180	22.727 25	15	0.909 090	0.227 275	0.002 840
6	216	27.272 70	18	1.090 908	0.272 730	0.003 408
7	252	31.818 15	21	1.272 726	0.318 185	0.003 976
8	288	36.363 60	24	1.454 544	0.363 640	0.004 544
9	324	40.909 05	27	1.636 362	0.409 095	0.005 112
10	360	45.454 50	30	1.818 180	0.454 550	0.005 680

FOOT; (FEET).

"Sub-multiples":

    inch(es)   link(s)

"Multiples":

    yard(s)   rod(s)   chain(s)   mile(s)

"One foot" in length is equal to:

    12 inches   1.515 152 links   0.333 333 yard

    0.060 606 rod   0.015 152 chain   0.000 189 mile

How to denote "foot; feet" as "metric measures":

"One foot" in length is equal to:

    0.304 8 meter   3.048 decimeters   30.48 centimeters

    304.8 millimeters   0.030 48 dekameter

    0.003 048 hectometer   0.000 304 8 kilometer

How to denote "foot; feet" as "metric decimals":

ft	m	dm	cm	mm
1	0.304 8	3.048	30.48	304.8
2	0.609 6	6.096	60.96	609.6
3	0.914 4	9.144	91.44	914.4
4	1.219 2	12.192	121.92	1 219.8
5	1.524 0	15.240	152.40	1 524.0
6	1.828 8	18.288	182.88	1 828.8
7	2.133 6	21.336	213.36	2 133.6
8	2.438 4	24.384	243.84	2 438.4
9	2.743 2	27.432	274.32	2 743.2
10	3.048 0	30.480	304.80	3 048.0

LINK.

(Surveyor's or: Gunter's).

"Sub-multiples:

    inch(es)

"Multiples:

    feet   yard(s)   chain(s)   mile(s)

"One link" in length is equal to:

    7.92 inches   0.66 foot   0.22 yard   0.04 rod

    0.01 chain   0.000 125 mile

How to denote "link" as "metric measures":

"One link" in length is equal to:

    0.201 168 meter   2.011 68 decimeters

    20.116 8 centimeters   201.116 8 millimeters

    0.020 116 8 dekameter   0.002 011 68 hectometer

    0.000 201 168 kilometer

INCH.

"Multiples":

    link(s)   foot; feet   yard(s)   rod(s)

    chain(s)   mile(s)

"One inch" in length is equal to:

    0.126 263 link   0.083 333 3 foot   0.027 777 78 yard

    0.005 051 rod   0.001 263 chain   0.000 016 mile

How to denote "inch" as "metric measures":

"One inch" in length is equal to:
0.025 4 meter   0.254 decimeter   2.54 centimers   25.400 mm
0.002 54 dekameter   0.000 254 hectometer   0.000 025 4 km

How to denote "inch(es) as "metric decimals":

in	m	dm	cm	mm
1	0.025 4	0.254	2.54	25.400
2	0.050 8	0.508	5.08	50.800
3	0.076 2	0.762	7.62	76.200
4	0.101 6	1.016	10.16	101.600
5	0.127 0	1.270	12.70	127.000
6	0.152 4	1.524	15.24	152.400
7	0.177 8	1.778	17.78	177.800
8	0.203 2	2.032	20.32	203.200
9	0.228 6	2.286	22.86	228.600
10	0.254 0	2.540	25.40	254.000

How to denote "inch fraction" as:

in	mm decimals		in decimals
1	25.400		1.000
1/2	12.700		0.5
1/4	6.350		0.25
1/8	3.175		0.125
1/16	1.588		0.062 5
1/32	0.794		0.031 25
1/64	0.397		0.015 625

"Tenth" of **"one inch"** denoted as **"millimeter(s) decimals"**:

in	mm
1/10	2.540
2/10	5.080
3/10	7.620
4/10	10.160
5/10	12.700
6/10	15.240
7/10	17.780
8/10	20.320
9/10	22.860
1	25.400

"Hundredth" of **"one inch"** denoted as **"millimeter(s) decimals"**:

in	mm
1/100	0.254
2/100	0.508
3/100	0.762
4/100	1.016
5/100	1.270
6/100	1.524
7/100	1.778
8/100	2.032
9/100	2.286
1/10	2.540

"Thousandth" of "one inch" denoted as "millimeter decimals":

in	mm
1/1 000	0.025 4
2/1 000	0.050 8
3/1 000	0.076 2
4/1 000	0.101 6
5/1 000	0.127 0
6/1 000	0.152 4
7/1 000	0.177 8
8/1 000	0.203 2
9/1 000	0.228 6
1/100	0.254 0

ROD.
(Also: "Pole" or: "Perch").

"Sub-multiples":

    inch(es)   link(s)   foot; feet   yard(s)

"Multiples":

    chain(s)   mile(s)

"One rod" in length is equal to:

    198 inches   25 links   16.5 feet

    5.5 yards   0.25 chain   0.003 125 mile

How to denote "rod" as "metric measures:

"One rod" in length is equal to:

5.029 2 meters   50.292 decimeters   502.92 centimeters

5 029.2 millimeters   0.502 92 dam   0.050 292 hm
0.005 029 2 km

CHAIN.

(Surveyor's or: Gunter's).

"Sub-multiples":

    inch(es)   link(s)   foot; feet   yard(s)   rod(s)

"Multiples":

    mile(s)

"One chain" in length is equal to:

    792 inches   100 links   66 feet   22 yards

    4 rods   0.012 5 mile

How to denote "chain" to "metric measures":

"One chain" in length is equal to:

    20.116 8 meters   201.168 decimeters

    2 011.68 centimeters   20 116.8 millimeters

    0.201 168 hectometer   0.020 116 8 kilometer

CHAIN.

(Engineer's or: Ramden's).

A line or tape of 100 links.

"One chain" in length is equal to:

    30.48 meters   equal to   100 feet

LINK.

(Engineer's or: Ramden's).

"One link" in length is equal to:

    0.305 meter   equal to   1 foot

FURLONG.

"One furlong" in length is equal to:

| 7 920 inches | 1 000 links | 660 feet | 220 yards |
| 40 rods | 10 chains | 0.125 mile | |

How to denote "furlong" as "metric measures":

"One furlong" in length is equal to:

201.168 meters	2 011.68 decimeters
20 116.8 centimeters	201 168 millimeters
20.116 8 dekameters	2.011 68 hectometers
0.201 168 kilometer	

MILE.
(Statute mile).

The "mile" is a measure of distance.

"Sub-multiples":

| inch(es) | link(s) | foot; feet | yard(s) |
| rod(s) | chain(s) | furlong(s) | |

"Multiples: none

"One mile" in length is equal to:

63 360 inches	8 000 links	5 280 feet
1 760 yards	320 rods	80 chains
8 furlongs		

How to denote "mile" as "metric" measures":

"One mile" in length is equal to:

1 609.344 meters	16 093.44 decimeters	160 934.4 centimeters
1 609 344 millimers	160.934 4 dekameters	
16.093 44 hectometers	1.609 344 kilometers	

How to denote "mile(s) as "metric decimals":

mi	km	m
1	1.609 344	1 609.344
2	3.218 688	3 218.688
3	4.828 032	4 828.032
4	6.437 376	6 437.376
5	8.046 720	8 046.720
6	9.656 064	9 656.064
7	11.265 408	11 265.408
8	12.874 752	12 874.752
9	14.484 096	14 484.096
10	16.093 440	16 093.440

INTERNATIONAL NAUTICAL MILE.

International Nautical Mile (INM) is a unit of distance at sea. This unit is now accepted in the U.S.A.
"INM" as "U.S. measurements":

    1 INM = 1.150 779 statute mile
    1 INM = 6 076.115 49 feet
"INM" as "metric measurements":

    1 INM = 1.852 kilometer
    1 INM = 1 852 meters
To convert "statute mile(s)" into "INM": multiply "statute mile(s)" by 0.868 976.
To convert "INM" into "statute mile(s)": multiply INM by 1.150 779 or: roughly; INM times 1 1/7

NAUTICAL MILE.

Also known as: geographical mile, air mile, etc.

Considered as 1/60 th. of a degree of the earth's equator.

"One nautical mile" = 6 080.2 feet

"One nautical mile" = 1 853.25 meters

KNOT.

The "knot" is a measure of speed equal to 1.151 6 statute
mile per hour or equal to one nautical mile per hour.
One knot is equal to 1.853.4 kilometer per hour (km/h).

Various "U.S." and"international" measurements.

3 marine nautical miles = 1 league

3 marine nautical miles = 5.559 75 kilometers

1 spanish legua nueva = 8000 yards

1 spanish legua nueva = 6687 meters

League (land)

A measure of distance about 2.42 to 4.6 statute miles but
usually considered approximately 3 miles or: 4 828 kilometers.

Point (typographically).

1 point = 0.013 837 inch or: 0.351 millimeter.

Mil.

1 mil = 0.001 inch or: 0.0254 millimeter.

Hand.

A unit of measurement, used to state the height of horses.

1 hand = 4 inches or: 10.16 centimeters.

Fathom.

1 fathom = 1.828 meters, 100 fathoms = 600 feet or: 0.1 nautical mile.

Cable's length.

1 cable's length = 120 fathoms or: = 720 feet.

7 1/3 cable's length = 1 nautical mile.

Swedish new mile.

1 swedish new mile = 6.213 7 miles.

1 swedish new mile = 10 kilometers.

"Swedish new mile" is also known as: norwegian and danish mie.

New geographic mile.

1 new geographic mile = 7.42 kilometers.

World Seamile.

1 world seamile = 1.852 kilometer, or: 1 nautical mile.

French Seamile.

1 french seamile = 3 INM, or: 1 league, or: 5.559 75 kilometers.

Equador grad.

1 equador grad = 15 geographic seamiles or: 1 degree,

or: 69 1/6 miles, or: 111.306 kilometers.

Meridian grad.

1 meridian grad = 60 seamiles (average) = 96.540 kilometers.

Russian werst.

1 russian werst = 1500 Arschinen, or: 500 saschen,

or: 1 166.64 yards, or: 1 066.78 meters.

MEASURES OF SURFACES.

The "square meter" is the principal and basic unit to
to designate the area(s) or surface(s).
"One square meter" (m^2) is an area or surface measuring
"one meter in length" and "one meter in width".
Each "sub-multiple" of the apropriate "square unit"
increases by 100 times. Established results are commonly
written with "three decimal fractions" but may be "rounded
off" for the reason of simplicity and convenience.

SQUARE METER.
(Basic "Unit").

"Sub-multiples":

square decimeter(s), square centimeter(s), square millimeter(s)
"One square meter" is equal to:

$$100 \ dm^2 \qquad 10 \ 000 \ cm^2 \qquad 1 \ 000 \ 000 \ mm^2$$

"Multiples":

square dekameter(s), square hectometer(s), square kilometer(s)
$100 \ m^2 = 1 \ dam^2$, $10 \ 000 \ m^2 = 1 \ hm^2$, $1 \ 000 \ 000 \ m^2 = 1 \ km^2$
How to denote "square meter" as "U.S. measurements":
"One square meter" is equal to:

1 550.003 inches^2	24.710 54 links^2
10.763 91 feet^2	1.195 990 yard^2
0.039 536 86 rod^2	0.002 471 105 4 chain^2
0.000 000 386 102 2 mile^2	

How to denote "square meter(s)" as "metric multiples":

m^2	dam^2	hm^2	km^2
1	0.01	0.000 1	0.000 001
2	0.02	0.000 2	0.000 002
3	0.03	0.000 3	0.000 003
4	0.04	0.000 4	0.000 004
5	0.05	0.000 5	0.000 005
6	0.06	0.000 6	0.000 006
7	0.07	0.000 7	0.000 007
8	0.08	0.000 8	0.000 008
9	0.09	0.000 9	0.000 009
10	0.10	0.001 0	0.000 010

How to denote "square meter(s)" as "metric sub-multiples":

m^2	dm^2	cm^2	mm^2
1	100	10 000	1 000 000
2	200	20 000	2 000 000
3	300	30 000	3 000 000
4	400	40 000	4 000 000
5	500	50 000	5 000 000
6	600	60 000	6 000 000
7	700	70 000	7 000 000
8	800	80 000	8 000 000
9	900	90 000	9 000 000
10	1 000	100 000	10 000 000

How to denote "square meter(s)" as "U.S. measurements":

m^2	in^2	$link^2$	ft^2	yd^2
1	1 550.003	24.710 54	10.763 91	1.195 990
2	3 100.006	49.421 08	21.527 82	2.391 980
3	4 650.009	74.131 62	32.291 73	3.587 970
4	6 200.012	98.842 16	43.055 64	4.783 960
5	7 750.015	123.552 70	53.819 55	5.979 950
6	9 300.018	148.263 24	64.583 46	7.175 940
7	10 850.021	172.973 78	75.347 37	8.371 930
8	12 400.024	197.684 32	86.111 28	9.567 920
9	13 950.027	222.394 86	96.875 19	10.763 910
10	15 500.030	247.105 40	107.639 10	11.959 900

How to denote "square meter(s)" as "U.S. measurements":

m^2	rod^2	ch^2	mi^2
1	0.039 536 86	0.002 471 054	0.000 000 386 102 2
2	0.079 073 72	0.004 942 108	0.000 000 772 204 4
3	0.118 610 58	0.007 413 162	0.000 001 158 306 6
4	0.158 147 44	0.009 884 216	0.000 001 544 408 8
5	0.197 684 30	0.012 355 270	0.000 001 930 511 0
6	0.237 221 16	0.014 826 324	0.000 002 316 613 2
7	0.276 758 02	0.017 297 378	0.000 002 702 715 4
8	0.316 294 88	0.019 768 432	0.000 003 088 817 6
9	0.355 831 74	0.022 239 486	0.000 003 474 919 8
10	0.395 368 60	0.024 710 540	0.000 003 861 022 0

SQUARE DECIMETER.

"Sub-multiples":

    square centimeter(s)   square millimeter(s)

"One square decimeter" is equal to:

    100 centimeters^2 10 000 millimeters^2

"Multiples":

    square meter(s)   square dekameter(s)

    square hectometer(s)   square kilometer(s)

How to denote "square decimeter" as "U.S. measures":

"One square decimeter" is equal to:

    15.500 3 inches^2 0.107 6 foot^2 0.011 959 9 yd^2

How to denote "square decimeter(s) as "metric sub-multiples":

dm^2	cm^2	mm^2
1	100	10 000
2	200	20 000
3	300	30 000
4	400	40 000
5	500	50 000
6	600	60 000
7	700	70 000
8	800	80 000
9	900	90 000
10	1 000	100 000

How to denote "square decimeter(s)" as "U.S. measurements":

dm^2	in^2	ft^2	yd^2
1	15.500 3	0.107 6	0.011 959 9
2	31.000 6	0.215 2	0.023 919 8
3	46.500 9	0.322 8	0.035 879 7
4	62.001 2	0.430 4	0.047 839 6
5	77.501 5	0.538 0	0.059 799 5
6	93.001 8	0.645 6	0.071 759 4
7	108.502 1	0.753 2	0.083 719 3
8	124.002 4	0.860 8	0.095 679 2
9	139.502 7	0.968 4	0.107 639 1
10	155.003 0	1.076 0	0.119 599 0

SQUARE CENTIMETER.

"Sub-multiple":

    square millimeter(s)

"One square centimeter" is equal to:

    100 square millimeters

"Multiples":

    square decimeter(s)   square meter(s)

    square dekameter(s)   square hectometer(s)

How to denote "square centimeter" as "U.S. measures":

"One square centimeter" is equal to:

    0.155 000 3 inch^2 or: roughly 1/16 th of one inch^2

    0.001 076 foot^2 0.000 119 599 yard^2

How to denote "square centimeter(s)" as a "metric sub-multiple":

cm^2	mm^2
1	100
2	200
3	300
4	400
5	500
6	600
7	700
8	800
9	900
10	1 000

How to denote "square centimeter(s)" as "U.S. measurements":

cm^2	in^2	ft^2
1	0.155 000 3	0.001 076
2	0.310 000 6	0.002 152
3	0.465 000 9	0.003 228
4	0.620 001 2	0.004 304
5	0.775 001 5	0.005 380
6	0.930 001 8	0.006 456
7	1.085 002 1	0.007 532
8	1.240 002 4	0.008 608
9	1.395 002 7	0.009 684
10	1.550 003 0	0.010 760

SQUARE MILLIMETER.

"Multiples":

    square centimeter(s)   square decimeter(s)

    square meter(s)   square dekameter(s)

    square hectometer(s)   square kilometer(s)

How to denote "square millimeter" as "U.S. measures":

"One square millimeter" is equal to:

    roughly 1/600 th of 1 $inch^2$ or: 0.002 $inch^2$

    1 mm^2 = 0.001 55 in^2

SQUARE DEKAMETER.

"One square dekameter" is equal to:

    100 m^2 10 000 dm^2 1 000 000 cm^2

How to denote "square dekameter" as "U.S. measurements":

"One square dekameter" is equal to:

    11.959 9 yd^2 1 076.391 ft^2 155 000.3 in^2

SQUARE HECTOMETER.

"One square hectometer" is equal to:

    100 square dekameters   10 000 square meters

How to denote " One square hectometer" as "U.S. measures":

    11 195.99 $yards^2$ 1 076 391.0 $feet^2$

SQUARE KILOMETER.

"One square kilometer" is equal to:

    100 square hectometers   10 000 square dekameters

    1 000 000 square meters

How to denote "kilometer^2" as "U.S. measurements":

"One square kilometer" is equal to:

    10 763 910.0 ft^2 1 119 599.0 yd^2 0.386 102 2 mi^2

SQUARE YARD.

"One square yard" is equal to:

    1 296.0 in^2 20.661 16 link^2 0.033 057 85 rod^2

    0.002 066 12 ch^2 0.000 000 322 830 mi^2

How to denote "yard^2" as "metric measurements":

"One square yard" is equal to:

    0.836 127 36 m^2 83.612 736 dm^2 8 361.273 6 cm^2

    836 127.36 mm^2 0.083 612 736 dam^2

    0.000 083 612 736 hm^2 0.000 000 083 612 736 km^2

How to denote "square yard(s)" as "metric measures":

yd^2	m^2	dm^2	cm^2	mm^2
1	0.836 127 36	83.61	8 361.273 6	8 361 273.6
2	1.672 254 72	167.23	16 722.547 2	16 722 547.2
3	2.508 382 08	250.84	25 083.820 8	25 083 820.8
4	3.344 509 44	334.45	33 445.094 4	33 445 094.4
5	4.180 636 80	418.06	41 806.368 0	41 806 368.0
6	5.016 764 16	501.68	50 167.641 6	50 167 641.6
7	5.852 891 52	585.29	58 528.915 2	58 528 915.2
8	6.689 018 88	668.90	66 890.188 8	66 890 188.8
9	7.525 146 24	752.51	75 251.462 4	75 251 462.4
10	8.361 273 60	836.13	83 612.736 0	83 612 736.0

How to denote "square yard(s)" as other "U.S. measurements".

yd^2	in^2	$link^2$	ft^2	rod^2
1	1 296	20.661 16	9	0.033 057 85
2	2 592	41.322 32	18	0.066 115 70
3	3 888	61.983 48	27	0.099 173 55
4	5 184	82.644 64	36	0.132 231 40
5	6 480	103.305 80	45	0.165 289 25
6	7 776	123.966 96	54	0.198 347 10
7	9 072	144.628 12	63	0.231 404 95
8	10 368	165.289 28	72	0.264 462 80
9	11 664	185.950 44	81	0.297 520 65
10	12 960	206.611 60	90	0.330 578 50

How to denote "square yard(s)" as other "U.S. measurements":

yd^2	ch^2	mi^2
1	0.002 066 12	0.000 000 322 830 6
2	0.004 132 24	0.000 000 645 661 2
3	0.006 198 36	0.000 000 968 491 8
4	0.008 264 48	0.000 001 291 322 4
5	0.010 330 60	0.000 001 614 153 0
6	0.012 396 72	0.000 001 936 983 6
7	0.014 462 84	0.000 002 259 814 2
8	0.016 528 96	0.000 002 582 644 8
9	0.018 595 08	0.000 002 905 475 4
10	0.020 661 20	0.000 003 228 306 0

SQUARE INCH.

"One square inch" is equal to:

$0.015\ 942\ 3\ link^2$ $0.006\ 944\ ft^2$

$0.000\ 771\ 605\ yd^2$ $0.000\ 025\ 5\ rod^2$

$0.000\ 001\ 594\ ch^2$ $0.000\ 000\ 000\ 249\ 1\ mi^2$

How to denote "square inch" as "metric measures":

"One square inch" is equal to:

$0.000\ 645\ 16\ meter^2$ $0.064\ 516\ decimeter^2$

$6.451\ 6\ centimeters^2$ $645.16\ millimeters^2$

$0.000\ 006\ 451\ 6\ dam^2$ $0.000\ 000\ 064\ 516\ hm^2$

$0.000\ 000\ 000\ 645\ 16\ km^2$

How to denote "square inch(es)" as "metric measures":

in^2	mm^2	cm^2	m^2
1	645.16	6.451 6	0.000 645 16
2	1 290.32	12.903 2	0.001 290 32
3	1 935.48	19.354 8	0.001 935 48
4	2 580.64	25.806 4	0.002 580 64
5	3 225.80	32.258 0	0.003 225 80
6	3 870.95	38.709 6	0.003 870 96
7	4 516.12	45.161 2	0.004 516 12
8	5 161.28	51.612 8	0.005 161 28
9	5 806.44	58.064 4	0.005 806 44
10	6 451.60	64.516 0	0.006 451 60

How to denote "square inch(es)" as other "U.S. measurements":

in^2	link^2	ft^2	yd^2
1	0.015 942 3	0.006 944	0.000 771 605
2	0.031 884 6	0.013 888	0.001 543 210
3	0.047 826 9	0.020 832	0.002 314 815
4	0.063 769 2	0.027 776	0.003 086 420
5	0.079 711 5	0.034 720	0.003 858 025
6	0.095 653 8	0.041 664	0.004 629 630
7	0.111 596 1	0.048 608	0.005 401 235
8	0.127 538 4	0.055 552	0.006 172 840
9	0.143 480 7	0.062 496	0.006 944 445
10	0.159 423 0	0.069 440	0.007 716 050

How to denote "square inch(es)" as other "U.S. measurements":

in^2	rod^2	ch^2	mi^2
1	0.000 025 5	0.000 001 594	0.000 000 000 249 1
2	0.000 051 0	0.000 003 188	0.000 000 000 498 2
3	0.000 076 5	0.000 004 782	0.000 000 000 747 3
4	0.000 102 0	0.000 006 376	0.000 000 000 996 4
5	0.000 127 5	0.000 007 970	0.000 000 001 245 5
6	0.000 153 0	0.000 009 564	0.000 000 001 494 6
7	0.000 178 5	0.000 011 158	0.000 000 001 743 7
8	0.000 204 0	0.000 012 752	0.000 000 001 992 8
9	0.000 229 5	0.000 014 346	0.000 000 002 241 9
10	0.000 255 0	0.000 015 940	0.000 000 002 491 0

SQUARE LINK.

"One square link" is equal to:

$62.726\ 4\ in^2$ $\qquad\qquad$ $0.435\ 6\ ft^2$

$0.048\ 4\ yd^2$ $\qquad\qquad$ $0.000\ 1\ ch^2$

$0.000\ 000\ 015\ 625\ mi^2$

How to denote "square link" as "metric measurements":

"One square link" is equal to:

$0.040\ 468\ 564\ 224\ m^2$ $\qquad$ $4.04\ dm^2$ "rounded off"

$404.685\ 642\ 24\ cm^2$ $\qquad$ $40\ 468.\ 564\ 224\ mm^2$

SQUARE FOOT; FEET.

"One square foot" is equal to:

$144\ in^2$ $\qquad$ $2.295\ 684\ link^2$ $\qquad$ $0.111\ 111\ 1\ yd^2$

$0.003\ 673\ 09\ rod^2$ $\qquad\qquad\qquad$ $0.000\ 229\ 568\ ch^2$

$0.000\ 000\ 035\ 870\ 06\ mi^2$

How to denote "square foot; feet" as "metric measurements":

"One square foot" is equal to:

$0.092\ 903\ 04\ m^2$ $\qquad\qquad$ $9.29\ dm^2$ "rounded off"

$929.030\ 4\ cm^2$ $\qquad\qquad$ $92\ 903.04\ mm^2$

How to denote "square foot; feet" as "metric measures":

ft^2	m^2	dm^2 "rounded off"	cm^2	mm^2
1	0.092 903 04	9.29	929.030 4	92 903.04
2	0.185 806 08	18.58	1 858.060 8	185 806.08
3	0.278 709 12	27.87	2 787.091 2	278 709.12
4	0.371 612 16	37.16	3 716.121 6	371 612.16
5	0.464 515 20	46.45	4 645.152 0	464 515.20
6	0.557 418 24	55.74	5 574.182 4	557 418.24
7	0.650 321 28	65.03	6 503.212 8	650 321.28
8	0.743 224 32	74.32	7 432.243 2	743 224.32
9	0.836 127 36	83.61	8 361.273 6	836 127.36
10	0.929 030 40	92.90	9 290.304 0	929 030.40

How to denote "square foot; feet" as other "U.S. measures":

ft^2	link^2	in^2	yd^2	rod^2	ch^2
1	2.295 684	144	0.11	0.003 673 09	0.000 229 568
2	4.591 368	288	0.22	0.007 346 18	0.000 459 136
3	6.887 052	432	0.33	0.011 019 27	0.000 688 704
4	9.182 736	576	0.44	0.014 692 36	0.000 918 272
5	11.478 420	720	0.55	0.018 365 45	0.001 147 840
6	13.774 104	864	0.66	0.022 038 54	0.001 377 408
7	16.069 788	1 008	0.77	0.025 711 63	0.001 606 976
8	18.365 472	1 152	0.88	0.029 384 72	0.001 836 544
9	20.661 156	1 296	1.00	0.033 057 81	0.002 066 112
10	22.956 840	1 440	1.11	0.036 730 90	0.002 295 680

SQUARE ROD.

(Also: square pole; square perch).

"One square rod; pole; perch" is equal to:

    39 204 in^2 625 links^2 272.25 ft^2 30.25 yd^2

    0.062 5 ch^2 0.000 009 765 625 mi^2

How to denote "square rod; pole; perch" as "metric measures":

"One square rod; pole perch" is equal to:

    25.292 852 64 m^2 252 928.526 4 cm^2

    252 928 526.4 mm^2

SQUARE CHAIN.

"One square chain" is equal to:

    627 264 in^2 10 000 links^2 4 356 ft^2

    484 yd^2 16 rods^2 0.000 156 25 mi^2

How to denote "square chain" as "metric measures":

"One square chain" is equal to:

    404.685 642 24 m^2

    404.7 m^2 "rounded off"

    404 685 6 cm^2

    0.000 404 7 km^2

How to denote "square chain(s)" as "metric measures":

ch^2	cm^2	m^2	km^2 (rounded off)
1	4 046 856	404.685 642 24	0.000 405
2	8 093 712	809.371 284 48	0.000 809
3	12 140 568	1 214.056 926 72	0.001 214
4	16 187 424	1 618.742 568 96	0.001 619
5	20 234 280	2 023.428 211 20	0.002 023
6	24 281 136	2 428.113 853 44	0.002 428
7	28 327 882	2 832.799 495 68	0.002 833
8	32 374 848	3 237.485 137 92	0.003 237
9	36 421 704	3 642.170 780 16	0.003 642
10	40 468 560	4 046.856 422 40	0.004 047

How to denote "square chain(s)" as other U.S. measures:

ch^2	rod^2	ft^2	$link^2$	yd^2
1	16	4 356	10 000	484
2	32	8 712	20 000	968
3	48	13 068	30 000	1 452
4	64	17 424	40 000	1 936
5	80	21 780	50 000	2 420
6	96	26 136	60 000	2 904
7	112	30 492	70 000	3 388
8	128	34 848	80 000	3 872
9	144	39 204	90 000	4 356
10	160	43 560	100 000	4 840

SQUARE BUILDING.

$$\text{One Building}^2 = 100 \text{ ft}^2$$

As "metric measurement":

$$\text{One Building}^2 = 9.290\ 304\ m^2$$

ANGULAR AND CIRCULAR MEASUREMENTS.

60 (") seconds = 1 minute (')

60 (') minutes = 1 degree (°)

90° degrees = 1 right angle (1 quadrant)

180° degrees = 1 straight angle

360° degrees = 1 circle (circumference)

CIRCULAR MILE.

$$1 \text{ circular mile} = 0.785\ 4\ mi^2$$

As "metric measurement":

$$1 \text{ circular mile} = 2.034\ 2\ km^2$$

SQUARE MILE.

"One square mile" is equal to:

4 014 489 600 in^2	64 000 000 links^2
27 878 400 ft^2	3 097 600 yd^2
102 400 rods^2	6 400 ch^2

How to denote "square mile" as "metric measurements":

"One square mile" is equal to:

2 589 988 110.3 cm^2	2 589 988.110 3 m^2
2.59 km^2 (rounded off)	

How to denote "square mile(s)" as "metric measures":

mi^2	cm^2	m^2	km^2 (rounded off)
1	25 899 881 103	2 589 988.11	2.59
2	51 799 762 206	5 179 976.22	5.18
3	77 699 643 309	7 769 964.33	7.77
4	103 599 524 412	10 359 952.44	10.36
5	129 499 405 515	12 949 940.55	12.95
6	155 399 286 618	15 539 928.66	15.54
7	181 299 167 721	18 129 916.77	18.13
8	207 199 048 824	20 719 904.88	20.72
9	233 098 929 927	23 309 892.99	23.31
10	258 998 811 030	25 899 881.10	25.90

How to denote "square mile(s)" as other "U.S. measurements":

mi^2	in^2	ft^2	yd^2
1	4 014 489 600	27 878 400	3 097 600
2	8 028 979 200	55 756 800	6 195 200
3	12 043 468 800	83 635 200	9 292 800
4	16 057 958 400	111 513 600	12 390 400
5	20 072 448 000	139 392 000	15 488 000
6	24 086 937 600	167 270 400	18 585 600
7	28 101 427 200	195 148 800	21 683 200
8	32 115 916 800	223 027 200	24 780 800
9	36 130 406 400	250 905 600	27 878 400
10	40 144 896 000	278 784 000	30 976 000

MEASURES OF AGRARIAN SURFACES.

In the "metric system", "are(s)", "hectare(s)" and "centi-
are(s)" are the proper and official terms to express the
definite surface(s) content(s) of open space(s) such as land(s)
field(s), forest(s), mining claim(s) and for a large variety
of other regional measure(s), but usually unoccupied areas.
"ARE" is the principal and basic unit and is as such adopted
to measure all agrarian terrains of the same kind as "are(s)".
"ARE" was originally adopted from the Latin Language where
it denoted an "area surface" or a "small territory".
The "are" has only one multiple the "hectare".
This expression originated in the Greek Language as "hecto"
and "hecaton" meaning "a hundred".
The "are" has as the only sub-multiple the "centiare"
(also called "centare).
As a word from the Latin Language "centi" (also "centum")
stands for "hundred".

ARE.

The "are" is the principal, and basic unit to measure
"agrarian surfaces".
"One are" is equal to:

    100 meter^2 100 centares   1/100 hectare

    1 are = 10 m on each side, also called "one dekameter^2"

    100 ares = 1 hectare

How to denote "are" as U.S. measures":

"One are" is equal to:

$155\ 000.3\ in^2$ $1\ 076.391\ ft^2$ $2\ 471.054\ links^2$

$119.599\ yd^2$ $0.247\ 105\ 4\ ch^2$ $0.024\ 710\ 54$ acre

$3.953\ 686\ rods^2$ $0.000\ 386\ 102\ 2\ mi^2$

How to denote "are(s)" as other "metric measures":

a	ca also: m^2	ha	dm^2	km^2
1	100	0.01	1 000 000	0.010
2	200	0.02	2 000 000	0.020
3	300	0.03	3 000 000	0.030
4	400	0.04	4 000 000	0.040
5	500	0.05	5 000 000	0.050
6	600	0.06	6 000 000	0.060
7	700	0.07	7 000 000	0.070
8	800	0.08	8 000 000	0.080
9	900	0.09	9 000 000	0.090
10	1 000	0.10	10 000 000	0.100

How to denote "are(s)" as U.S. measurements:

a	in^2	$links^2$	ft^2	yd^2
1	155 000.3	2 471.054	1 076.391	119.599
2	310 000.6	4 942.108	2 152.782	239.198
3	465 000.9	7 413.162	3 229.173	358.797
4	620 001.2	9 884.216	4 305.564	478.396
5	775 001.5	12 355.270	5 381.955	597.995
6	930 001.8	14 826.324	6 458.346	717.594
7	1 085 002.1	17 297.378	7 534.737	837.193
8	1 240 002.4	19 768.432	8 611.128	956.792
9	1 395 002.7	22 239.486	9 687.519	1 076.391
10	1 550 003.0	24 710.540	10 763.910	1 195.990

How to denote "are(s)" as U.S. measurements:

a	ch^2	acre	$rods^2$	mi^2
1	0.247 105 4	0.024 710 54	3.953 686	0.000 386 102 2
2	0.494 210 8	0.049 421 08	7.907 372	0.000 772 204 4
3	0.741 316 2	0.074 131 62	11.861 058	0.001 158 306 6
4	0.988 421 6	0.098 842 16	15.814 744	0.001 544 408 8
5	1.235 527 0	0.123 552 70	19.768 430	0.001 830 511 0
6	1.482 632 4	0.148 263 24	23.722 116	0.002 316 613 2
7	1.729 737 8	0.172 973 78	27.675 802	0.002 702 715 4
8	1.976 843 2	0.197 684 32	31.629 488	0.003 088 817 6
9	2.223 948 6	0.222 394 86	35.583 174	0.003 474 919 8
10	2.471 054 0	0.247 105 40	39.536 860	0.003 861 022 0

CENTIARE.

The "centiare" is the only "sub-multiple" of the "are".
"One centiare" is equal to:

   1 meter^2

How to denote "centiare" as "U.S. measures":
"One centiare" is equal to:

   1 550.003 in^2 10.763 91 ft^2 1.195 990 yd^2

   0.039 536 86 rods^2 0.002 471 054 ch^2

   24.710 54 links^2 0.000 247 105 4 acre

HECTARE.

The "hectare" is the "multiple" of the "are":
"One hectare" is equal to:

   100 are: 100 m on each side.

   10 000 m^2

   10 000 centiares

   0.1 km^2

How to denote "hectare" as "U.S. measures":
"One hectare" is equal to:

   2.471 054 acre(s)   11 959.9 yd^2 107 639.1 ft^2

It would be illogical to use the other square measures.

DEKARE.

"One dekare" is equal to:

   10 a   1 000 m^2

SQUARE LEAGUA.

(Old spanish land measure).

"U.S. measure":

    4.438 acre

"metric measure":

    17 808 m^2

ACRE FOOT.

"One acre foot" is the amount of any substance (water, soil,
etc.) needed to make a level area of one acre one foot higher.

    1 acre foot = 1 613 yd^3 as "U.S. measure".

    1 acre foot = 1 234 m^3 as "metric measure".

ACRE INCH.

"One acre inch" is the 12 th part of "one acre foot".

acre in	yd^3	ft^3	m^3
1	134.4	3 630	107.05
2	268.8	7 260	214.10
3	403.2	10 890	321.15
4	537.6	14 520	428.20
5	672.0	18 150	535.25
6	806.4	21 780	642.30
7	940.8	25 410	749.35
8	1 075.2	29 040	856.40
9	1 209.6	32 670	963.45
10	1 344.0	36 300	1 070.50

"U.S. acre(s)" denoted as: "metric": hectare(s), are(s) and centare(s):

U.S. acre(s)	metric "rounded off". hectare(s)	ares	centares
1	0.4	40	4 047
2	0.8	80	8 094
3	1.2	121	12 141
4	1.6	161	16 188
5	2.0	202	20 235
6	2.4	242	24 282
7	2.8	283	28 329
8	3.2	323	32 376
9	3.6	364	36 423
10	4.0	404	40 470

SECTION OF LAND.

"One section of land" is equal to:

"U.S. measures":

1 mi^2 or: 640 acres

"metric measures": "rounded off".

2.59 km^2 or: 259 hectares

TOWNSHIP.

"One township" is equal to:

"U.S. measures":

6 mi^2 or: 36 sections of land; or: 3 840 acres.

"metric measures": "rounded off".

93.24 km^2 or: 9 324 hectares.

How to denote "decare" as "U.S. measures":

"One decare" is equal to:

    0.247 1 acre   1 195.99 yd^2

HECTOMETER.

"One hectometer" is equal to:

    10 000 m^2 100 dam^2 100 a   1 ha

How to denote "hectometer" as "U.S. measures":

"One hectometer" is equal to:

    2.471 acre   11 959.9 yd^2

ACRE.

In the U.S. System, "acre" is the proper and generalized term to express the content of the open space surfaces. A degree of comparison with agricultural measures in the "Metric system" is almost impossible. In order to obtain an accurate measured result, smaller denominations must be applied for computations.

           1 acre = 208.76 ft on each side

"One acre" is equal to:

    6 272 640 in^2 100 000 $links^2$ 43 560 ft^2

    4 840 yd^2 160 $rods^2$ 10 ch^2 0.001 562 5 mi^2

How to denote "acre" as "metric measures":

"One acre"is equal to:

    40.468 564 224 a   4 046.856 422 4 ca

    0.404 685 642 24 ha (0.405 ha roughly "rounded off".

How to denote "U.S. acre(s)" as "metric hectare(s)":

acre(s)	hectare(s)
1	0.404 69
2	0.809 37
3	1.214 06
4	1.618 74
5	2.023 43
6	2.428 11
7	2.832 80
8	3.237 49
9	3.642 17
10	4.046 86

How to denote "metric hectare(s)" as "U.S. acre(s)":

hectare(s)	acre(s)
1	2.471 1
2	4.942 1
3	7.413 2
4	9.884 2
5	12.355 3
6	14.826 3
7	17.297 4
8	19.768 4
9	22.239 5
10	24.710 5

CUBIC MEASURES.

The "cubic meter" is the principal and basic unit to
designate the volume contained.

"One cubic meter" (m^3) is a cube measuring one meter
on each side.

Measured results are commonly written with three decimal
fractions but may be "rounded off".

CUBIC METER.
Unit = 1 cubic meter (m^3).

"Sub-multiples":

    cubic decimeter(s)   cubic centimeter(s)

    cubic millimeter(s)

"Multiples":

    The "cubic meter" has no multiples.

How to denote "cubic meter" as "U.S. measurements":

"One cubic meter" is equal to:

    61 023.74 in^3 35.314 67 ft^3 1.307 950 619 yd^3

"One cubic meter" is equal to:

    1 000 cubic decimeters   1 000 000 cubic centimeters

    1 000 000 000 cubic millimeters

- 60 -

How to denote "cubic meter(s)" as "metric sub-multiples":

m^3	mm^3	cm^3	dm^3
1	1 000 000 000	1 000 000	1 000
2	2 000 000 000	2 000 000	2 000
3	3 000 000 000	3 000 000	3 000
4	4 000 000 000	4 000 000	4 000
5	5 000 000 000	5 000 000	5 000
6	6 000 000 000	6 000 000	6 000
7	7 000 000 000	7 000 000	7 000
8	8 000 000 000	8 000 000	8 000
9	9 000 000 000	9 000 000	9 000
10	10 000 000 000	10 000 000	10 000

How to denote "cubic meter(s)" as "U.S. measurements":

m^3	in^3	ft^3	yd^3
1	61 023.74	35.314 67	1.307 950 619 3
2	122 047.48	70.629 34	2.615 901 238 6
3	183 071.22	105.944 01	3.923 851 857 9
4	244 094.96	141.258 68	5.231 802 477 2
5	305 118.70	176.573 35	6.539 753 096 5
6	366 142.44	211.888 02	7.847 703 715 8
7	427 166.18	247.202 69	9.155 654 335 1
8	488 189.92	282.517 36	10.463 604 954 4
9	549 214.66	317.832 03	11.771 555 573 7
10	610 237.40	353.146 70	13.079 506 193 0

CUBIC DECIMETER.

"One cubic decimeter" = the 1 000 th part of 1 m^3

"One cubic decimeter" is equal to:

    1 000 000 mm^3 1 000 cm^3 0.001 m^3

How to denote "cubic decimeter" as "U.S. measurements":

"One cubic decimeter" is equal to:

    61.023 74 in^3 0.035 314 67 ft^3 0.001 307 951 yd^3

CUBIC CENTIMETER.

"One cubic centimeter" = the 1 000 000 th part of 1 m^3

"One cubic centimeter" is equal to:

    1 000 mm^3 0.001 dm^3 0.000 001 m^3

How to denote "cubic centimeter" as "U.S. measurements":

    0.061 023 74 in^3 0.000 035 315 ft^3 0.000 001 308 yd^3

CUBIC MILLIMETER.

"One cubic millimeter" = the 1 000 000 000 th part of 1 m^3

    1 000 mm^3 = 1 cm^3

How to denote "cubic millimeter" as "U.S. measurement":

"One cubic millimeter" is equal to:

    0.000 061 in^3

CUBIC YARD.

"One cubic yard" is equal to:

    46 656 in^3 27 ft^3

How to denote "cubic yard" as "metric measurements":

"One cubic yard" is equal to:

    0.764 554 857 984 m^3 764.554 858 984 dm^3

    764 554.857 984 cm^3

How to denote "cubic yard(s)" as "metric measures":

yd^3	cm^3	dm^3	m^3
		"r o u n d e d o f f"	
1	764 554.857 984	764.9	0.765
2	1 529 109.715 968	1 529.1	1.529
3	2 293 664.573 952	2 293.7	2.294
4	3 058 219.431 936	3 058.2	3.058
5	3 822 774.289 920	3 822.8	3.823
6	4 587 329.147 904	4 587.3	4.587
7	5 351 884.005 888	5 351.9	5.352
8	6 116 438.863 872	6 116.4	6.116
9	6 880 993.721 856	6 880.1	6.881
10	7 645 548.579 840	7 645.5	7.646

How to denote "cubic yard(s)" as other "U.S. measures":

yd^3	ft^3	in^3
1	27	46 656
2	54	93 312
3	81	139 968
4	108	186 624
5	135	233 280
6	162	279 936
7	189	326 592
8	216	372 248
9	243	419 904
10	270	466 560

CUBIC FOOT (FEET).

"One cubic foot" is equal to:

    1 728 in^3 0.037 037 04 yd^3

    27 ft^3 = 1 yd^3

    128 ft^3 = 1 cord of firewood

How to denote "cubic foot" as "metric measures":

"One cubic foot" is equal to:

    28 316 846.592 mm^3 28 316.846 592 cm^3

    28.316 847 dm^3 0.028 316 847 m^3

    35.316 ft^3 = 1 m^3

How to denote "cubic foot; feet" as other "U.S. measures:

ft^3	in^3	yd^3
1	1 728	0.037
2	3 456	0.074
3	5 184	0.111
4	6 912	0.148
5	8 640	0.185
6	10 368	0.222
7	12 096	0.259
8	13 824	0.296
9	15 552	0.333
10	17 280	0.370

How to denote "cubic foot; feet" as "metric measures":

ft^3	cm^3	dm^3	m^3 "rounded off"
1	28 316.846 592	28.316 847	0.028
2	56 633.693 184	56.633 694	0.056
3	84 950.539 776	84.950 541	0.084
4	113 267.386 368	113.267 388	0.113
5	141 584.232 960	141.584 235	0.141
6	169 901.079 552	169.901 082	0.169
7	198 217.926 144	198.217 929	0.198
8	226 534.772 736	226.534 776	0.226
9	254 851.619 328	254.851 623	0.254
10	283 168.465 920	283.168 470	0.283

CUBIC INCH.

"One cubic inch" is equal to:

0.000 578 704 ft^3 0.000 021 433 yd^3

How to denote "cubic inch" as "metric measures":

"One cubic inch" is equal to:

16 387.064 mm^3 16.387 064 cm^3

0.016 387 064 dm^3 0.000 016 387 064 m^3

How to denote "cubic inch(es)" as other "U.S. measures":

in^3	ft^3	yd^3
1	0.000 578 704	0.000 021 433
2	0.001 157 408	0.000 042 866
3	0.001 736 112	0.000 064 299
4	0.002 314 816	0.000 085 732
5	0.002 893 520	0.000 107 165
6	0.003 472 224	0.000 128 598
7	0.004 050 928	0.000 150 031
8	0.004 629 632	0.000 171 464
9	0.005 208 336	0.000 192 897
10	0.005 787 040	0.000 214 330

How to denote "cubic inch(es)" as "metric measures":

in^3	mm^3	cm^3	dm^3	m^3
1	16 387.064	16.387 064	0.016 387	0.000 016 387
2	32 774.128	32.774 128	0.032 774	0.000 032 774
3	49 161.192	49.161 192	0.049 161	0.000 049 161
4	65 548.256	65.548 256	0.065 548	0.000 065 548
5	81 935.320	81.935 320	0.081 935	0.000 081 935
6	98 322.384	98.322 384	0.098 322	0.000 098 322
7	114 709.448	114.709 448	0.114 709	0.000 114 709
8	131 096.512	131.096 512	0.131 096	0.000 131 096
9	147 483.576	147.483 576	0.147 483	0.000 147 483
10	163 870.640	163.870 640	0.163 870	0.000 163 870

PERCH OF STONE.

"One perch" of stone or brick is as a "U.S. measure":

    $16\frac{1}{2}$ ft long, $1\frac{1}{2}$ ft wide, 1 ft high.

    or: 24 3/4 ft^3 = 1 perch of stone or brick.

How to denote "perch of stone or brick as "metric measures":
"One perch of stone or brick" is equal to:

    5.029 2 m long, 0.457 2 m wide, 0.304 8 m high.

    or: 0.72 m^3

BOARD FOOT; FEET.

The "board foot; feet" is a unit of measure for lumber in
the United States. It denotes the contents of a board
1 foot square and 1 inch thick.

    1 board foot = 2 398.8 cubic centimeters.

MEASURE OF FIREWOOD.

Firewood as a solid source of material to generate heat, is
in the "metric system" measured and computed with the same
method as "cubic measures". However, it must be considered
that there are always empty spaces between piled logs, and
one (1) measured STERE never will equal exactly the contents
of one (1^3) cubic meter.
The word STERE originated in the Greek language as "stereo"
or "solid".

The STERE is the principal and basic unit, and has two
multiples, the "dekastere" and the "hectostere".
The two sub-multiples of the STERE are "decistere" and
"centistere".
The multiples, and sub-multiples are almost not in use to
measure firewood, solely by computing STERE(S) into U.S.
measurements or U.S. measurements into STERE(S).
A continuous sequence of ordinary numbers is generally used
to denote the amount of STERE(S).
For example: 200 steres are commonly referred to as being
200 steres, instead of being 2 hectosteres. This is also
customery concerning the multiples "dekastere(s)" and
"hectostere(s)".
The sub-multiples "decistere(s)" and "centistere(s)" are
written after the decimal point following immediately
the "full stere(s)".

<u>For example:</u> 1 stere, 6 decisteres, 3 centisteres is written

as being: 1.63 steres.

How to denote "stere" as "metric measures":

1 stere is:	1 m^3 (1 m x 1 m x 1 m)
1 decistere is:	1/10 th of one stere
1 centistere is:	1/100 th of one stere
1 hectostere is:	100 steres or: 100 m^3
1 decastere is:	10 steres or: 10 m^3

How to denote "stere" as "U.S. measures":

1 stere = 2½ cord feet of firewood.

3.6 steres = 1 cord of firewood.

1 decastere = 10 steres or: 2 3/4 cords of firewood.

1 hectostere = 100 steres or: 28 cords of firewood.

How to measure values of "firewood" in the "U.S. system":

The measurements of "firewood" are in the "U.S. system" known

as "cord(s)". One "cord" is assumed as being a pile of logs,

8 ft long, 4 ft wide and 4 ft high; or: equal to 128 ft^3

1 cord is: 8 cord feet

1 cord is: 128 ft^3

1 cord foot is: 16 ft^3

How to denote "cord" as "metric measures":

1 cord = 3.624 steres

1 cord foot = 4.5 decisteres

27 ft^3 = 1 stere

2 3/4 cord feet = 1 stere

MEASURES OF WEIGHT.

The "gram" is the principal and basic unit, however the
"multiples" are used to denote weights larger than a "gram".
The "sub-multiples" of the unit "gram" are:

decigram	(10 to one gram)
centigram	(100 to one gram)
milligram	(1 000 to one gram)
microgram	(1 000 000 to one gram)

The "multiples" of the unit "gram" are:

dekagram	(10 grams)
hectogram	(100 grams)
kilogram	(1 000 grams)
ton (metric)	(1 000 000 grams)

In commercial use all weights are used in gram, kilogram or
metric tons, depending largely on the size of the weight.

GRAM.

The basic unit for measuring weights is the "gram".
(1) one gram is the weight of (1) one cm^3 of distilled water
at 4 $^\circ$Celsius.
1 000 grams is 1 kilogram and equal to the weight of (1) liter
of distilled water at 4 $^\circ$Celsius.

How to denote "gram" as "U.S. weights":

"One gram" is equal to:

    15.432 36 grains

    0.771 617 9 apothecaries' scruple

    0.643 014 9 pennyweight

    0.564 383 4 avoirdupois-dram

    0.257 206 0 apothecaries' dram

    0.035 273 96 avoirdupois-ounce

    0.032 150 75 apothecaries' or troy ounce

    0.002 679 229 apothecaries' or troy pound

    0.002 204 623 avoirdupois pound

How to denote "gram" as other "metric weights":

g	dg	cg	mg	kg
1	10	100	1 000	0.001
2	20	200	2 000	0.002
3	30	300	3 000	0.003
4	40	400	4 000	0.004
5	50	500	5 000	0.005
6	60	600	6 000	0.006
7	70	700	7 000	0.007
8	80	800	8 000	0.008
9	90	900	9 000	0.009
10	100	1 000	10 000	0.010

How to denote "gram(s)" as "U.S. weights":

g	scr	gr	gr	dwt
1	0.771 617 9	15.432 36	15 7/16-	0.643 014 9
2	1.543 235 8	30.864 72	30 7/8-	1.286 029 8
3	2.314 853 7	46.297 08	46 2/7+	1.929 044 7
4	3.086 471 6	61.729 44	61 5/7+	2.572 059 6
5	3.858 089 5	77.161 80	77 1/6-	3.215 074 5
6	4.629 707 4	92.594 16	92 3/5-	3.858 089 4
7	5.401 325 3	108.026 52	108 1/40+	4.501 104 3
8	6.172 943 2	123.458 88	123 9/20+	5.144 119 2
9	6.944 561 1	138.891 24	138 9/10-	5.787 134 1
10	7.716 179 0	154.323 60	154 5/15-	6.430 149 0

The equivalents in "decimals" are mathematically exact.
The equivalents in common "fractions" are as near as such
fractions, now in use, permit.
Thus for the common fractions the minus sign (-) means
"a trifle" less and the plus sign (+) means "a trifle" more.

g	dr	oz tr	lb tr
1	0.257 206 0	0.032 150 75	0.002 679 229
2	0.514 412 0	0.064 301 50	0.005 358 458
3	0.771 618 0	0.096 452 25	0.008 037 687
4	1.028 824 0	0.128 603 00	0.010 716 916
5	1.286 030 0	0.160 753 75	0.013 396 145
6	1.543 236 0	0.192 904 50	0.016 075 374
7	1.800 442 0	0.225 055 25	0.018 754 603
8	2.057 648 0	0.257 206 00	0.021 433 832
9	2.314 854 0	0.289 356 75	0.024 113 061
10	2.572 060 0	0.321 507 50	0.026 792 290

How to denote "gram(s)" as "U.S. weights":

g	dr avdp	oz avdp	lb avdp
1	0.564 383 4	0.035 273 96	0.002 204 623
2	1.128 766 8	0.070 547 92	0.004 409 246
3	1.693 150 2	0.105 831 88	0.006 613 869
4	2.257 533 6	0.141 095 84	0.008 818 492
5	2.821 917 0	0.176 369 80	0.011 023 115
6	3.386 300 4	0.211 643 76	0.013 227 738
7	3.950 683 8	0.246 917 72	0.015 432 361
8	4.515 067 2	0.282 191 68	0.017 636 984
9	5.079 450 6	0.317 465 64	0.019 841 607
10	5.643 834 0	0.352 739 60	0.022 046 230

DECIGRAM.

1 decigram is equal to:

    1 tenth of one gram

   10 centigrams

  100 milligrams

For equivalents in decimals etc. see "gram's", "grain's" etc.

How to denote "decigram(s)" as "U.S. weights":

dg	grain(s)	grain(s)
1	1.543 2	1 10/18-
2	3.086 4	3 1/2+
3	4.629 7	4 5/8+
4	6.172 9	6 1/16+
5	7.716 1	7 7/10+
6	9.259 4	9 1/4+
7	10.802 6	10 4/5+
8	12.345 8	12 7/20+
9	13.889 1	13 22/25+
10	15.432 3	15 7/16-

MICROGRAM.

1 microgram equals 0.000 001 gram

CENTIGRAM.

1 centigram is equal to:

1/100 th of one gram	0.01 gram
10 milligrams	1/10 th decigram

How to denote "centigram" as "U.S. weights":

1 centigram is equal to 0.154 3 grain.

For equivalents in decimals etc. see "gram's".

How to denote "centigram(s)" as "U.S. weights":

cg	grain	grain
1	0.154 3	3/20+
2	0.308 6	3/10+
3	0.462 9	7/15-
4	0.617 2	5/8-
5	0.771 6	14/18-
6	0.925 9	14/15-
7	1.080 2	1 1/2-
8	1.234 5	1 7/30+
9	1.388 9	1 7/18+
10	1.543 0	1 10/18-

MILLIGRAM.

The "milligram" is a sub-multiple of the gram.

(1) one milligram is the 1 000 ths. part of one gram.

(10) ten milligrams is (1) one centigram.

1 milligram = 0.000 001 kilogram.

How to denote "milligram" as "U.S. weights":

"One milligram" is equal to:

    0.015 432 gr   0.000 643 015 dwt

    0.000 564 383 dr avdp 0.000 035 274 oz avdp

    0.000 032 151 oz tr   0.000 002 679 lb tr

    0.000 002 205 lb avdp

How to denote "milligram(s)" as "U.S. weights":

mg	grain	grain
1	0.015 4	1/60-
2	0.030 8	1/30-
3	0.046 2	1/20-
4	0.061 7	1/15-
5	0.077 1	3/40+
6	0.092 5	9/100+
7	0.108 0	2/18-
8	0.123 4	1/8-
9	0.138 8	11/80+
10	0.154 3	3/20+

For equivalents in decimals etc. see "gram".

DEKAGRAM.

1 decagram is equal to: 10 grams   100 decigrams

How to denote "dekagram" as "U.S. weights":

1 decagram is equal to: 0.352 7 oz av$_{dp}$ 0.321 2 oz tr

HECTOGRAM.

1 hectogram is equal to: 100 grams   10 decagrams

How to denote "hectogram" as "U.S. weight":

1 hectogram is equal to: 2.680 lb tr

MYRIAGRAM. (obsolete; see page 12).

1 myriagram is equal to: 10 kilograms   10 000 grams

How to denote "myriagram" as "U.S. weight":

1 myriagram is equal to: 26.8 lb tr

KILOGRAM.

"kilo" in the metric system means a thousand times a given unit.

"kilogram" is a measure of weight meaning a thousand grams. In ordinary trade, weights are expressed as "kilogram".

1 kilogram is equal to:

      1 000 grams

      100 decigrams

       10 hectograms

      1 000 000 milligrams

      0.001 metric ton

How to denote "kilogram" as "U.S. weights":

1 kilogram is equal to:

   15 432.36 grains

      771.617 9 apothecaries' scruples

      643.014 9 pennyweights

      564.383 4 avoirdupois drams

      267.206 0 apothecaries' drams

       35.273 96 avoirdupois ounces

       32.150 75 apothecaries' or troy ounces

        2.679 229 apothecaries' or troy pounds

        2.204 623 avoirdupois pounds

        0.022 046 23 short hundredweight

        0.001 102 311 short ton

        0.000 094 207 long ton

How to denote "kilogram(s)" as other "metric weights":

kg	mg	hg	dg	g	t
1	1 000 000	10	100	1 000	0.001
2	2 000 000	20	200	2 000	0.002
3	3 000 000	30	300	3 000	0.003
4	4 000 000	40	400	4 000	0.004
5	5 000 000	50	500	5 000	0.005
6	6 000 000	60	600	6 000	0.006
7	7 000 000	70	700	7 000	0.007
8	8 000 000	80	800	8 000	0.008
9	9 000 000	90	900	9 000	0.009
10	10 000 000	100	1 000	10 000	0.010

How to denote "kilogram(s)" as "U.S. weights":

kg	grain(s)	scr	dwt	dr avdp
1	15 432.36	771.617 9	643.014 9	564.383 4
2	30 864.72	1 543.235 8	1 286.029 8	1 128.766 8
3	46 297.08	2 314.853 7	1 929.044 7	1 693.150 2
4	61 729.44	3 086.471 6	2 572.059 6	2 257.533 6
5	77 161.80	3 858.089 5	3 215.074 5	2 821.917 0
6	92 594.16	4 629.707 4	3 858.089 4	3 386.300 4
7	108 026.52	5 401.325 3	4 501.104 3	3 950.683 8
8	123 458.88	6 172.943 2	5 144.119 2	4 515.067 2
9	138 891.24	6 944.561 1	5 787.134 1	5 079.450 6
10	154 323.60	7 716.179 0	6 430.149 0	5 643.834 0

How to denote "kilogram(s)" as "U.S. weights":

kg	dram avdp	oz avdp	lb avdp	oz tr
1	257.206 0	35.273 96	2.204 623	32.150 75
2	514.412 0	70.547 92	4.409 246	64.301 50
3	771.618 0	105.821 88	6.613 869	96.452 25
4	1 028.824 0	141.095 84	8.818 492	128.603 00
5	1 286.030 0	176.369 80	11.023 115	160.753 75
6	1 543.236 0	211.643 76	13.227 738	192.904 50
7	1 800.442 0	246.917 72	15.432 361	225.055 25
8	2 057.648 0	282.191 68	17.636 984	257.206 00
9	2 314.854 0	317.465 64	19.841 607	289.356 75
10	2 572.060 0	352.739 60	22.046 230	321.507 50

How to denote "kilogram(s)" as "U.S. weights":

kg	lb tr	cwt	short ton	long ton
1	2.679 229	0.022 046 23	0.001 102 311	0.000 094 207
2	5.358 458	0.044 092 46	0.002 204 622	0.000 188 114
3	8.037 687	0.066 138 69	0.003 306 933	0.000 282 621
4	10.716 916	0.088 184 92	0.004 409 244	0.000 376 828
5	13.396 145	0.110 231 15	0.005 511 555	0.000 471 035
6	16.075 374	0.132 277 38	0.006 613 866	0.000 565 242
7	18.754 603	0.154 323 61	0.007 716 177	0.000 659 449
8	21.433 832	0.176 369 84	0.008 818 488	0.000 753 656
9	24.113 061	0.198 416 07	0.009 920 799	0.000 847 863
10	26.792 290	0.220 462 30	0.011 023 110	0.000 942 070

<u>TONNE</u> or:——→ <u>TON (metric)</u>.

1 ton = 1 000 kilograms

1 ton = 1 000 000 grams

How to denote "ton (metric)" as "U.S. weights":

1 ton "metric" is equal to:

    35 273.96 oz avdp

    32 150.75 oz tr

    22 046 23 short cwt

    2 679.229 lbs tr

    2 204.623 lbs avdp

      1.102 311 short ton

How to denote "ton(s) metric" as other "metric weights":

t	kg	g
1	1 000	1 000 000
2	2 000	2 000 000
3	3 000	3 000 000
4	4 000	4 000 000
5	5 000	5 000 000
6	6 000	6 000 000
7	7 000	7 000 000
8	8 000	8 000 000
9	9 000	9 000 000
10	10 000	10 000 000

How to denote "ton(s) metric" as "U.S. weights":

t	long ton's	short ton's	short cwt	lbs tr
1	0.984 206 5	1.102 311	22.046 23	2 679.23
2	1.968 413 0	2.204 622	44.092 46	5 358.46
3	2.952 619 5	3.306 933	66.138 69	8 037.69
4	3.936 826 0	4.409 244	88.184 92	10 716.91
5	4.921 032 5	5.511 555	110.231 15	13 396.14
6	5.905 239 0	6.613 866	132.277 38	16 075.37
7	6.889 445 5	7.716 177	154.323 61	18 754.60
8	7.873 652 0	8.818 488	176.370 04	21 433.83
9	8.857 858 5	9.920 799	198.416 07	24 113.06
10	9.842 065 0	11.023 110	220.462 30	26 792.28

How to denote "ton's metric" as "U.S. weights":

t	oz tr	lbs avdp	oz avdp
1	32 150.75	2 204.623	35 273.96
2	64 301.50	4 409.246	70 547.92
3	96 452.25	6 613.869	105 821.88
4	128 603.00	8 818.492	141 095.84
5	160 753.75	11 023.115	176 369.80
6	192 904.50	13 227.738	211 643.76
7	225 055.25	15 432.361	246 917.72
8	257 206.00	17 636.984	282 181.68
9	289 356.75	19 841.607	317 465.64
10	321 507.50	22 046.230	352 739.60

KILOTON.

1 kiloton = 1 000 metric tons or: 984.207 U.S. long tons.
Used as a unit to express the energy of thermonuclear
weapons (T.N.T.)

CENTNER.

A old hundredweight of various European countries.

1 centner = 50 kilograms.

PFUND.

A old weight of various European countries.

1 pfund = 30 lot = 300 quentchen or: 500 grams ($\frac{1}{2}$ kilogram)

QUINTAL.

"metric weights"	"U.S. weights"
1 quintal = 100 kilograms	220.462 lbs avdp
10 quintals = 1 ton	267.920 lbs tr

MILLIER or TONNEAU TON.

1 millier or tonneau ton equals:

"metric weights"	"U.S. weights"
1 000 000 grams	2 204.6 lbs avdp
1 000 kilograms	2 679.2 lbs tr
1 ton	

MEASURE OF VALUE.

CARAT.

1 carat = 200 milligrams = 3.086 U.S. grains
1 carat is the fineness of gold alloy = 1/24 th part.

GRAIN.

How to denote "grain" as "metric weights":

1 grain = 64.798 91 mg   1 grain = 0.000 064 799 kg

1 grain = 0.064 798 91 g   7 000 grains = 453.59 g

How to denote "grain" as other "U.S. weights":

1 grain= 0.05 scruple   0.016 666 67 apothecaries' dram

0.036 571 43 dr avdp   0.002 285 71 oz avdp

0.041 666 67 dwt   0.000 142 857 lb avdp

0.000 173 611 lbs tr   0.002 083 33 oz tr

How to denote "grain" as "metric weights":

grain	g	mg	grain	g	mg
1	0.064 800	64.800	1/30	0.002 160	2.160
1/2	0.032 400	32.400	1/40	0.001 620	1.620
1/3	0.021 600	21.600	1/50	0.001 290	1.290
1/4	0.016 200	16.200	1/60	0.001 080	1.080
1/5	0.012 900	12.900	1/80	0.000 810	0.810
1/6	0.010 800	10.800	1/100	0.000 648	0.640
1/7	0.009 200	9.200	1/120	0.000 540	0.540
1/8	0.008 100	8.100	1/125	0.000 518	0.510
1/10	0.006 400	6.400	1/130	0.000 498	0.490
1/12	0.005 400	5.400	1/140	0.000 463	0.460
1/15	0.004 320	4.320	1/150	0.000 432	0.430
1/16	0.004 050	4.050	1/160	0.000 405	0.400
1/18	0.003 600	3.600	1/180	0.000 360	0.360
1/20	0.003 240	3.240	1/200	0.000 324	0.320
1/25	0.002 590	2.590	1/250	0.000 259	0.259

PENNYWEIGHT.

How to denote "pennyweight" as other "U.S. weights":
"One pennyweight" is equal to:

    24 grains   0.4 dram

    1.2 scruples   0.877 143 dram avdp

    0.054 857 14 oz avdp   0.05 oz tr

    0.004 166 667 lbs tr   0.003 428 571 lbs avdp

How to denote "pennyweight" as "metric weights":
"One pennyweight" is equal to:

    1 555.173 84 mg   1.555 173 84 g

    0.001 551 738 4 kg

SCRUPLE.

How to denote "scruple" as other "U.S. weights":
"One scruple" is equal to:

    20 grains   0.833 33 3 dwt

    0.731 428 6 dram avdp   0.333 333 3 dram

    1 dram = 3 scruples   0.045 714 29 oz avdp

    0.041 666 67 oz tr   0.003 472 222 lbs tr

    0.002 857 143 lbs avdp

How to denote "scruple" as "metric weights":
"One scruple" is equal to:

    1 295.978 2 mg

      1.295 978 2 g

      0.001 295 978 kg

DRAM APOTHECARIES'.

How to denote "dram apothecaries'" as other "U.S. weights":

"One dram apothecaries'" is equal to:

60 grains	3 scruples	2.5 dwt
2.194 286 dr avdp		0.137 142 9 oz avdp
0.125 oz tr		0.010 416 67 lbs tr

How to denote "dram apothecaries'" as "metric weights":

"One dram apothecaries'" is equal to:

3 887.934 6 mg   3.887 934 6 g   0.003 887 934 6 kg

OUNCE TROY.

How to denote "ounce troy" as other "U.S. weights":

"One ounce troy" is equal to:

480 grains	20 dwt	24 scruples
8 drams	17.554 29 dr avdp	0.068 571 43 lbs avdp
1.097 143 oz avdp		0.083 333 333 lbs tr

12 oz tr = 1 lbs tr or is equal to: 240 dwt

How to denote "ounce troy" as "metric weights":

"One ounce troy" is equal to:

31 103.476 8 mg

31.103 476 8 g

0.031 103 476 8 kg

How to denote "ounce(s) troy" as other "U.S. weights":

oz tr	grain(s)	scr	dwt	dram(s)	lbs tr
1	480	24	20	8	0.083 33
2	960	48	40	16	0.166 66
3	1 440	72	60	24	0.249 99
4	1 920	96	80	32	0.333 32
5	2 400	120	100	40	0.416 65
6	2 880	144	120	48	0.499 98
7	3 360	168	140	56	0.583 31
8	3 840	192	160	64	0.666 64
9	4 320	216	180	72	0.749 97
10	4 800	240	200	80	0.833 30

How to denote "ounce(s) troy" as other "U.S. weights":

oz tr	dram avdp	oz avdp	lbs avdp
1	17.554 29	1.097 143	0.068 571 43
2	35.108 58	2.194 286	0.137 142 86
3	52.662 87	3.291 429	0.205 714 29
4	70.217 16	4.388 572	0.274 285 72
5	87.771 45	5.485 715	0.342 857 15
6	105.325 74	6.582 858	0.411 428 58
7	122.880 03	7.680 001	0.480 000 01
8	140.434 32	8.777 144	0.548 571 44
9	157.988 61	9.874 287	0.617 142 87
10	175.542 90	10.971 430	0.685 714 30

How to denote "ounce(s) troy" as "metric weights":

oz tr	mg	g	kg
1	31 103.476 8	31.103 476 8	0.031 103 476 8
2	62 206.953 6	62.206 953 6	0.062 206 953 6
3	93 310.430 4	93.310 430 4	0.093 310 430 4
4	124 413.907 2	124.413 907 2	0.124 413 907 2
5	155 517.384 0	155.517 384 0	0.155 517 384 0
6	186 620.860 8	186.620 860 8	0.186 620 860 8
7	217 724.337 6	217.724 337 6	0.217 724 337 6
8	248 827.814 4	248.827 814 4	0.248 827 814 4
9	279 931.291 2	279.931 291 2	0.279 931 291 2
10	311 034.768 0	311.034 768 0	0.311 034 768 0

APOTHECARIES' or: TROY POUND.

How to denote "apothecaries' or: troy pound" as other

"U.S. weights":

"One apothecaries' or: troy pound" is equal to:

    5 760 grains   288 scr   240 dwt

    210.651 4 dram avdp   13.165 oz avdp

    0.822 857 1 lbs avdp   96 drams tr

    12 oz tr

How to denote "apothecaries' or: troy pound" as "metric weights":

"One apothecaries' of: troy pound" is equal to:

    373 241.721 6 mg   373.241 721 6 g

    0.373 241 722 16 kg   0.000 373 241 722 16 metric ton

How to denote "apothecarie's or: troy pound(s) as other "U.S. weights":

lbs tr	oz tr	dram(s)	dwt	scr	lbs av dp
1	12	96	240	288	0.822 857 1
2	24	192	480	576	1.645 714 2
3	36	288	720	864	2.468 571 3
4	48	384	960	1 152	3.291 428 4
5	60	480	1 200	1 440	4.114 285 5
6	72	576	1 440	1 728	4.937 142 6
7	84	672	1 680	2 016	5.759 999 7
8	96	768	1 920	2 304	6.582 856 8
9	108	864	2 160	2 592	7.405 713 9
10	120	960	2 400	2 880	8.228 571 0

How to denote "apothecaries' or: troy pound(s) as other "U.S. weights":

lbs tr	oz avdp	dram(s) av	grain(s)
1	13.165 71	210.651 4	5 760
2	26.331 42	421.302 8	11 520
3	39.497 13	631.954 2	17 280
4	52.662 84	842.605 6	23 040
5	65.828 55	1 053.257 0	28 800
6	78.994 26	1 263.908 4	34 560
7	92.159 97	1 474.559 8	40 320
8	105.325 68	1 685.211 2	46 080
9	118.491 39	1 895.862 6	51 840
10	131.657 10	2 106.514 0	57 600

How to denote "apothecaries' or: troy pound(s)"as
"metric weights":

lbs tr	mg	g	kg
1	373 241.721 6	373.241 721 6	0.373 241 721 6
2	764 483.443 2	746.483 443 2	0.746 483 443 2
3	1 119 725.164 8	1 119.725 164 8	1.119 725 164 8
4	1 492 966.886 4	1 492.966 886 4	1.492 966 886 4
5	1 866 208.608 0	1 866.208 608 0	1.866 208 608 0
6	2 239 450.329 6	2 239.450 329 6	2.239 450 329 6
7	2 612 612.051 2	2 612.692 051 2	2.612 692 051 2
8	2 985 933.772 8	2 985.933 772 8	2.985 933 772 8
9	3 359 175.494 4	3 359.175 494 4	3.359 175 494 4
10	3 732 417.216 0	3 732.417 216 0	3.732 417 216 0

DRAM AVOIRDUPOIS.

How to denote "dram avoirdupois" as other "U.S. weights":

"One dram avoirdupois" is equal to:

27.343 75 grains   1.367 187 scruples   1.139 323 dwt

0.455 729 2 drams   0.062 5 oz avdp   0.056 961 5 oz tr

0.004 747 179 lbs tr   0.003 906 25 lbs avdp

16 drams av = 1 oz avdp   27 11/32 grains

How to denote "dram avoirdupois" as "metric weights":

"One dram avoirdupois" is equal to:

1 771.845 195 mg

1.771 845 195 g

0.001 771 845 195 kg

- 89 -

How to denote "dram(s) avoirdupois" as other "U.S. weights":

dram(s) avdp	grain(s)	scruple(s)	dwt	dram(s) tr
1	27.343 75	1.367 187 5	1.139 323	0.455 729 2
2	54.687 50	2.734 375 0	2.278 646	0.911 458 4
3	82.031 25	4.101 562 5	3.417 969	1.367 187 6
4	109.375 00	5.468 750 0	4.557 292	1.822 916 8
5	136.718 75	6.835 937 5	5.696 615	2.278 646 0
6	164.062 50	8.203 125 0	6.835 938	2.734 374 2
7	191.406 25	9.570 312 5	7.975 261	3.190 104 4
8	218.750 00	10.937 500 0	9.114 584	3.645 833 6
9	246.093 75	12.304 687 5	10.253 907	4.101 562 8
10	273.437 50	13.671 875 0	11.393 230	4.557 292 0

How to denote "dram(s) avoirdupois" as other "U.S. weights":

dram(s) avdp	oz tr	lbs tr	oz avdp	lbs avdp
1	0.056 966 15	0.004 747 179	0.062 5	0.003 906 25
2	0.113 932 30	0.009 494 358	0.125 0	0.007 812 50
3	0.170 898 45	0.014 241 537	0.187 5	0.011 718 75
4	0.227 864 60	0.018 988 716	0.250 0	0.015 625 00
5	0.284 830 75	0.023 735 895	0.312 5	0.019 531 25
6	0.341 796 90	0.028 483 074	0.375 0	0.023 437 50
7	0.398 763 05	0.033 230 253	0.437 5	0.027 343 75
8	0.455 729 20	0.037 977 432	0.500 0	0.031 250 00
9	0.512 695 35	0.042 724 611	0.562 5	0.035 156 25
10	0.569 661 50	0.047 471 790	0.625 0	0.039 062 50

How to denote "dram(s) avoirdupois" as "metric weights":

dram(s) av dp	mg	g	kg
1	1 771.845 195	1.771 845 195	0.001 771 845 195
2	3 543.690 390	3.543 690 390	0.003 543 690 390
3	5 315.535 585	5.315 535 585	0.005 315 535 585
4	7 087.380 780	7.087 380 780	0.007 087 380 780
5	8 859.225 975	8.859 225 975	0.008 859 225 975
6	10 631.071 170	10.631 071 170	0.010 631 071 170
7	12 402.916 365	12.402 916 365	0.012 402 916 365
8	14 174.761 560	14.174 761 560	0.014 174 761 560
9	15 946.606 755	15.946 606 755	0.015 946 606 755
10	17 718.451 950	17.718 451 950	0.017 718 451 950

OUNCE AVOIRDUPOIS.

"One ounce avoirdupois" is equal to:

16 drams avdp	4 375 grains	18.229 17 dwt
7.291 667 drams tr	0.911 458 3 oz tr	
0.062 5 lbs avdp	0.000 625 s cwt	
0.000 031 25 short ton	0.000 027 902 long ton	

16 oz avdp = 1 lbs avdp

How to denote "ounce avoirdupois" as "metric weights":

"One ounce avoirdupois" is equal to:

28 349.523 125 mg   28.349 523 125 g

0.028 349 523 kg   0.000 028 350 metric ton

POUND AVOIRDUPOIS.

When it is necessary to distinguish the avoirdupois weights from the troy weights, the word "avoirdupois" or the abbreviation "avdp" should be used in combination with the name or abbreviation of the two different units.

How to denote "pound avoirdupois" as other "U.S. weights":
"One pound avoirdupois" is equal to:

16 oz avdp	7 000 grains	256 drams
291.667 dwt	14.583 33 oz tr	0.01 s cwt
1.215 278 lbs tr	0.000 5 short ton	

0.000 446 429 long ton

112 lbs avdp = 1 cwt (long or: gross)

100 lbs avdp = 1 cwt

2 240 lbs avdp = 1 long ton

How to denote "pound avoirdupois" as "metric weights":
"One pound avoirdupois" is equal to:

453 592.37 mg	453.592 37 g
0.453 592 37 kg	0.000 453 592 37 metric ton

How to denote "pound avoirdupois" as other "U.S. weights":

lbs avdp	oz avdp	dram(s)	grain(s)	s cwt	short ton
1	16	256	7 000	0.01	0.000 5
2	32	512	14 000	0.02	0.001 0
3	48	768	21 000	0.03	0.001 5
4	64	1 024	28 000	0.04	0.002 0
5	80	1 280	35 000	0.05	0.002 5
6	96	1 536	42 000	0.06	0.003 0
7	112	1 792	49 000	0.07	0.003 5
8	128	2 048	56 000	0.08	0.004 0
9	144	2 304	63 000	0.09	0.004 5
10	160	2 560	70 000	0.10	0.005 0

How to denote "pound avoirdupois" as other "U.S. weights":

lbs avdp	long ton	dwt	oz tr	lbs tr
1	0.000 446 429	291.666 7	14.583 33	1.215 278
2	0.000 892 858	583.333 4	29.166 66	2.430 556
3	0.001 339 287	875.000 1	43.749 99	3.645 834
4	0.001 785 716	1 166.666 8	58.333 32	4.861 112
5	0.002 232 145	1 458.333 5	72.916 65	6.076 390
6	0.002 678 574	1 750.000 2	87.499 98	7.291 668
7	0.003 125 003	2 041.666 9	102.083 31	8.506 946
8	0.003 571 432	2 333.333 6	116.666 64	9.722 224
9	0.004 017 861	2 625.000 3	131.249 97	10.937 502
10	0.004 464 290	2 916.667 0	145.833 30	12.152 780

How to denote "pound(s) avoirdupois" as "metric weights":

lbs avdp	mg	g	kg	metric ton
1	453 592.37	453.592 37	0.453 592 37	0.000 453 592
2	907 184.74	907.184 74	0.907 184 74	0.000 907 184
3	1 360 777.11	1 360.777 11	1.360 777 11	0.001 360 776
4	1 814 369.48	1 814.369 48	1.814 369 48	0.001 814 368
5	2 267 961.85	2 267.961 85	2.267 961 85	0.002 267 960
6	2 721 554.22	2 721.554 22	2.721 554 22	0.002 721 552
7	3 175 146.59	3 175.146 59	3.175 146 59	0.003 175 144
8	3 628 738.96	3 628.738 96	3.628 738 96	0.003 628 736
9	4 082 331.33	4 082.331 33	4.082 331 33	0.004 082 328
10	4 535 923.70	4 535.923 70	4.535 923 70	0.004 535 920

HUNDREDWEIGHT.

When the terms "hundredweight" and "ton" are used, it commonly
denotes the "100 lbs avdp cwt" or the "2 000 lbs avdp ton".
These units may be denoted "net or"short" when necessary.
Give at all times "short", "gross" or "long cwt" information.

How to denote "hundredweight" as other "U.S. weights":
"One hundredweight" is equal to:

    1 600 oz avdp   100 lbs avdp   0.05 short ton

    0.044 642 86 long ton

    20 short hundredweights = 1 short ton = 2 000 lbs tr

How to denote "hundredweight" as "metric weights":

"One hundredweight" is equal to: 45.359 237 kg
    0.045 359 237 metric ton

GROSS, also: LONG HUNDREDWEIGHT.

How to denote "gross hundredweight" as other "U.S. weights":

"One gross (long) hundredweight" is equal to:

    2 240 lbs avdp   20 gross cwt = 1 long ton

How to denote "gross hundredweight" as "metric weights":

"One gross (long) hundredweight" is equal to:

    907.184 740 kg

TON (short): (net)

How to denote "ton (short)" as other "U.S. weights":

"One ton (short) is equal to:

    0.892 857 1 long ton   2 430.50 lbs tr   29 166 oz tr

    2 000 lbs avdp   32 000 oz avdp   20 short cwt

How to denote "ton (short)" as "metric weights":

"One ton (short)" is equal to:

    907.184 74 kg   907 184.74 g   0.907 184 74 metric t

How to denote "ton (short)" as other "U.S. weights":

short ton	lbs tr	lbs avdp	short cwt	long ton
1	2 430.5	2 000	20	0.892 857 1
2	4 861.0	4 000	40	1.785 714 2
3	7 291.5	6 000	60	2.678 571 3
4	9 722.0	8 000	80	3.571 428 4
5	12 152.5	10 000	100	4.464 285 5
6	14 583.0	12 000	120	5.357 142 6
7	17 013.5	14 000	140	6.249 999 7
8	19 444.0	16 000	160	7.142 856 8
9	21 874.5	18 000	180	8.035 713 9
10	24 305.0	20 000	200	8.928 571 0

How to denote "ton (short)" as "metric weights":

short ton	g	kg	metric ton
1	907 184.74	907.184 74	0.907 184 74
2	1 814 369.48	1 814.369 48	1.814 369 48
3	2 721 554.22	2 721.554 22	2.721 554 22
4	3 628 738.96	3 628.738 96	3.628 738 96
5	4 535 923.70	4 535.923 70	4.535 923 70
6	5 443 108.44	5 443.108 44	5.443 108 44
7	6 350 293.18	6 350.293 18	6.350 293 18
8	7 257 477.92	7 257.477 92	7.257 477 92
9	8 164 662.66	8 164.662 66	8.164 662 66
10	9 071 847.40	9 071.847 40	9.071 847 40

LONG TON (gross).

The "gross" or "long ton" also "hundredweight" are used as a measure for weight in the U.S., to a limited extent, usually in very restricted industrial fields. These units are the same as the British "ton and/or hundredweight".

How to denote "long ton" as other "U.S. weights":

"One long ton" is equal to:

  2 722.22 lbs tr   32 666 64 oz tr   2 240 lbs avdp

How to denote "long ton" as "metric weights":

"One long ton" is equal to:

  1 016 046 908.8 g   1 016.046 908 8 kg

  1.016 046 908 9 metric ton

How to denote "long ton(s) (gross)" as other "U.S. weights":

long ton	lbs avdp	lbs tr	short cwt	short ton
1	2 240	2 722.22	22.4	1.12
2	4 480	5 444.44	44.8	2.24
3	6 720	8 166.66	67.2	3.36
4	8 960	10 888.88	89.6	4.48
5	11 200	13 611.10	112.0	5.60
6	13 440	16 333.32	134.4	6.72
7	15 680	19 055.54	156.8	7.84
8	17 920	21 777.76	179.2	8.96
9	20 160	24 499.98	201.6	10.08
10	22 400	27 222.20	224.0	11.20

How to denote "long ton(s) (gross)" as "metric weights":

long ton	g	kg	ton metric
1	1 016 046 908.8	1 016.046 908 8	1.016 046 908 8
2	2 032 093 817.6	2 032.093 817 6	2.032 093 817 6
3	3 048 140 726.4	3 048.140 726 4	3.048 140 726 4
4	4 064 187 635.2	4 064.187 635 2	4.064 187 635 2
5	5 080 234 544.0	5 080.234 544 0	5.080 234 544 0
6	6 096 281 452.8	6 096.281 452 8	6.096 281 452 8
7	7 112 328 361.6	7 112.328 361 6	7.112 328 361 6
8	8 128 375 270.4	8 128.375 270 4	8.128 375 270 4
9	9 144 422 179.2	9 144.422 179 2	9.144 422 179 2
10	10 160 469 088.0	10 160.469 088 0	10.160 469 088 0

ASSAY TON.

One assay ton = 29.167 grams (see "gram" for other compar-
isons). Used for assaying purposes only, the "assay ton"
of 2 000 lbs avdp bears the oz tr, or weight in mg of valuable
metall (gold, silver, etc.), obtained from "one assay ton"
of ore.

STONE.

How to denote "stone" as "U.S. weights":
"One stone" is equal to:

    14 lbs avdp (rounded off)   17.02 lbs tr (rounded off)

How to denote "stone" as a "metric weight":
"One stone" is equal to:

    6.351 kg

KEG.

How to denote "keg" as a "U.S. weight":
"One keg" is equal to:

    100 lbs avdp (usually the weight of nail's).

How to denote "keg" as a "metric weight":
"One keg" is equal to:

    45.4 kg (rounded off).

QUARTER.

"One quarter" as "U.S. weight's" = 2 stones = 28 lbs avdp

                                  34.4 lbs tr
                                  rounded off

"One quarter" as a "metric weight" = 12.702 kg

MEASURES OF CAPACITY.

The "liter" is in the "METRIC SYSTEM" the principal and basic
unit for liquid substances.
For purposes of conveniences, the instruments pertaining to
"liter" are mostly in the shape of cylinders.
"One liter" of pure water is equal to "one cubic-decimeter"
and weights "one kilogram".

Unit = 1 liter.

"Sub-multiple":

   sub-multiple = milliliter (1 000 to one liter)

"Multiple": none

(obsolete; see page 12).
obsolete "sub-multiple" is deciliter (10 to one liter)
obsolete "sub-multiple" is centiliter (100 to one liter)
obsolete "multiple" is dekaliter (10 liter's)
obsolete "multiple" is hectoliter (100 liter's)
obsolete "multiple" is kiloliter (1 000 liter's)

(obsolete; see page 12).

LITER.

(basic unit)

"One liter" = 1 kilogram of pure water.

"One liter" = 1 000 cm^3

"One liter" = 1 dm^3

"submultiples": (obsolete; see page 12).

   milliliter(s)   centiliter(s)   deciliter(s)

"One liter" is equal to:

   1 000 milliliters   100 centiliters   10 deciliters

"multiples":

   dekaliter(s)   hectoliter(s)   kiloliter(s)

   10 liters = 1 dekaliter   100 liters = 1 hectoliter

        1 000 liters = 1 kiloliter

How to denote "liter" as "U.S. measures":

"One liter" is equal to:

0.035 314 67 ft^3	61.023 74 in^3
1.816 166 dry pint	0.908 083 dry quart
0.028 377 59 dry bushel	0.113 510 37 peck (liquid and/or dry)
16.231 19 minim's	270.519 88 liquid drams
33.814 02 liquid ounces	8.453 06 gill's
2.113 376 liquid pints	1.056 688 liquid quarts

0.264 172 05 liquid gallons

0.946 352 946 liter is "one liquid quart"

0.473 176 473 liter is "one liquid pint"

½ liter is slightly more as "one liquid pint".

How to denote "liter(s)" as "metric multiples":

liter(s)	dekaliter	hectoliter	kiloliter
1	0.1	0.01	0.001
2	0.2	0.02	0.002
3	0.3	0.03	0.003
4	0.4	0.04	0.004
5	0.5	0.05	0.005
6	0.6	0.06	0.006
7	0.7	0.07	0.007
8	0.8	0.08	0.008
9	0.9	0.09	0.009
10	1.0	0.10	0.010

(obsolete;
see page 12).

How to denote "liter(s)" as "metric sub-multiples":

liter(s)	milliliter	centiliter	deciliter
1	1 000	100	10
2	2 000	200	20
3	3 000	300	30
4	4 000	400	40
5	5 000	500	50
6	6 000	600	60
7	7 000	700	70
8	8 000	800	80
9	9 000	900	90
10	10 000	1 000	100

(obsolete;
see page 12).

How to denote "liter(s)" as "U.S. measures":

liter(s)	minim	gill	dram liquid	ounce liquid
1	16 231.19	8.453 742	270.519 8	33.814 97
2	32 462.38	16.907 484	541.039 6	67.629 94
3	48 693.57	25.361 226	811.559 4	101.444 91
4	64 924.76	33.814 968	1 082.079 2	135.259 88
5	81 155.95	42.268 710	1 352.599 0	169.074 85
6	97 387.14	50.722 452	1 623.118 8	202.889 82
7	113 618.33	59.176 194	1 893.638 6	236.704 79
8	129 849.52	67.629 936	2 164.158 4	270.519 76
9	146 080.71	76.083 678	2 434.678 2	304.334 73
10	162 311.90	84.537 420	2 705.198 0	338.149 70

How to denote "liter(s)" as "U.S. measures":

liter(s)	pint liquid	quart liquid	gallon liquid
1	2.113 436	1.056 718	0.264 179 4
2	4.226 872	2.113 436	0.528 358 8
3	6.340 308	3.170 154	0.792 538 2
4	8.453 744	4.226 872	1.056 717 6
5	10.567 180	5.283 590	1.320 897 0
6	12.680 616	6.340 308	1.585 076 4
7	14.794 052	7.397 026	1.849 255 8
8	16.907 488	8.453 744	2.113 435 2
9	19.020 924	9.510 462	2.377 614 6
10	21.134 360	10.567 180	2.641 794 0

How to denote "liter(s)" as "U.S. measures":

liter(s)	peck liquid	peck or pint dry	quart dry
1	0.113 514	1.816 217	0.908 108
2	0.227 028	3.632 434	1.816 216
3	0.340 542	5.448 651	2.724 324
4	0.454 056	7.264 868	3.632 432
5	0.567 570	9.081 085	4.540 540
6	0.681 084	10.897 302	5.448 648
7	0.794 598	12.713 519	6.356 756
8	0.908 112	14.529 736	7.264 865
9	1.021 626	16.345 953	8.172 972
10	1.135 140	18.162 170	9.081 080

How to denote "liter(s)" as "U.S. measures":

liter(s)	bushel dry	in^3	ft^3
1	0.028 378	61.025 45	0.035 315 66
2	0.056 756	122.050 90	0.070 631 32
3	0.085 134	183.076 35	0.105 946 98
4	0.113 512	244.101 80	0.141 262 64
5	0.141 890	305.127 25	0.176 578 30
6	0.170 268	366.152 70	0.211 893 96
7	0.198 646	427.178 15	0.247 209 62
8	0.227 024	488.203 60	0.282 525 28
9	0.255 402	549.229 05	0.317 840 94
10	0.283 780	610.254 50	0.353 156 60

DEKALITER. (obsolete; see page 12).

"One dekaliter" is a measure of capacity equal to 10 liters.

How to denote "dekaliter" as "U.S. measures":

"One dekaliter" is equal to:

 2.642 liquid gallons   0.283 784 dry bushels

How to denote "dekaliter(s)" as "U.S. measures":

dekaliter(s)	pint dry	quart dry	peck dry	bushel dry
1	18.162 17	9.081 084	1.135 136	0.283 784
2	36.324 34	18.162 168	2.270 272	0.567 568
3	54.486 51	27.243 252	3.405 408	0.851 352
4	72.646 68	36.324 336	4.540 544	1.135 136
5	90.810 85	45.405 420	5.675 680	1.418 920
6	108.973 02	54.486 504	6.810 816	1.702 704
7	127.135 19	63.567 588	7.945 952	1.986 488
8	145.297 36	72.648 672	9.081 088	2.270 272
9	163.459 53	81.729 756	10.216 224	2.554 056
10	181.621 70	90.810 840	11.351 360	2.837 840

HECTOLITER. (obsolete; see page 12).

"One hectoliter" is a measure of capacity equal to 100 liters.

How to denote "hectoliter" as "U.S. measures":

"One hectoliter" is equal to:

 26.418 liquid gallons   2.837 7 dry bushels

How to denote "hectoliter(s)" as "U.S. measures":

hectoliter(s)	bushel dry	gallon liquid	
1	2.837 74	26.418	(obsolete; <u>see</u> page 12).
2	5.675 48	52.836	
3	8.513 23	79.254	
4	11.350 97	105.672	
5	14.188 71	132.090	
6	17.026 45	158.508	
7	19.864 20	184.926	
8	22.701 94	211.344	
9	25.539 68	237.762	
10	28.377 40	264.180	

How to denote "hectoliter(s)" as "U.S. agrarian measures":

hectoliter(s) per acre	dry bushel(s) "per acre"	
1	1.148 40	(obsolete; <u>see</u> page 12).
2	2.296 80	
3	3.445 19	
4	4.593 59	
5	5.741 99	
6	6.890 39	
7	8.038 79	
8	9.187 19	
9	10.335 58	
10	11.484 01	

KILOLITER. (obsolete; see page 12).

"One kiloliter" is a measure of capacity equal to 1 000 liters.

"One kiloliter" is equal to:

1 000 liters	1 000 kg of pure water
1 metric ton of pure water	1 m^3 of water
100 dekaliters	10 hectoliters

How to denote "kiloliter" as "U.S. measures":

"One "kiloliter" is equal to:

264.18 liquid gallons	1.308 yd^3

PECK (DRY). (obsolete; see page 12).

"One "peck (dry)" is equal to:

0.25 bushel	2 gallons	8 dry quarts
16 dry pints	537.605 in^3	

4 dry pecks = 1 dry bushel

How to denote "peck (dry)" as "metric measures":

"One "peck (dry)" is equal to:

8.809 521 liters	88.095 deciliters
8 809.521 centiliters	0.880 952 1 dekaliter

How to denote "dry peck(s)" as "metric measures":

peck(s) dry	liters	deciliters (obsolete, see page 12)	centiliters
1	8.809 521	88.095 21	8 809.521
2	17.619 042	176.190 42	17 619.042
3	26.428 563	264.285 63	26 428.563
4	35.238 084	352.380 84	35 238.084
5	44.047 605	440.476 05	44 047.605
6	52.857 126	528.571 26	52 857.126
7	61.666 647	616.666 47	61 666.647
8	70.476 168	704.761 68	70 476.168
9	79.285 689	792.856 89	79 285.689
10	88.095 210	880.952 10	88 095.210

PINT (DRY).

"One dry pint" is equal to:

    0.062 5 dry peck   0.015 625 dry bushel

    33.600 313 5 in^3

    2 dry pints = 1 dry quart

    16 dry pints = 1 dry peck

How to denote "dry pint" as "metric measures":

"One dry pint" is equal to:

    0.055 059 5 decaliter   0.550 595 liter

    550.595 centiliter   5.505 95 deciliter

    550.595 cm^3

How to denote "dry pint(s)" as "metric measures":

pint(s) dry	liter	deciliter (obsolete, see page 12)	centiliter also: cm^3
1	0.550 595	5.505 95	550.595
2	1.101 190	11.011 90	1 101.190
3	1.651 785	16.517 85	1 651.785
4	2.202 380	22.023 80	2 202.380
5	2.752 975	27.529 75	2 752.975
6	3.303 570	33.035 70	3 303.570
7	3.854 165	38.541 65	3 854.165
8	4.404 760	44.047 60	4 404.760
9	4.955 355	49.553 55	4 955.355
10	5.505 950	55.059 50	5 505.950

QUART (DRY).

"one "dry quart" is equal to:

2 dry pints   0.125 dry pecks   0.031 25 dry bushel

67.200 625 in^3 8 dry quarts = 1 dry peck

How to denote "dry quart" as a "metric measure":

"One dry quart" is equal to:

1.101 19 liter

SHALDRON.

"One shaldron" = 86 dry bushels or: 3 030.48 liters

PINT (LIQUID).

"One liquid pint" is equal to:

    0.250 dry and liquid quart   4 liquid gills

    16 liquid ounces   7 680 minims

    28.875 in^3 2 4 liquid pints = 1 liquid quart

How to denote "liquid pint" as "metric measures":

"One liquid pint" is equal to:

    0.473 16 liter   4.731 6 deciliter, (obsolete, see page 12)

    47.316 centiliter (also: cm^3) 473.16 milliliter
    (obsolete, see page 12)

How to denote "liquid pint(s)" as "metric measures":

pint(s) liquid	liter	milliliter
1	0.473 163 2	473.163 2
2	0.946 326 4	946.326 4
3	1.419 489 6	1 419.489 6
4	1.892 652 8	1 892.652 8
5	2.365 816 0	2 365.816 0
6	2.838 979 2	2 838.979 2
7	3.312 142 4	3 312.142 4
8	3.785 305 6	3 785.305 6
9	4.258 468 8	4 258.468 8
10	4.731 632 0	4 731.632 0

How to denote "liquid pint(s)" as other "U.S. measures":

pint(s) liquid	gallon liquid	quart liquid	ounce liquid	dram liquid	minim liquid	in^3
1	0.125	0.25	16	128	7 680	28.875
2	0.250	0.50	32	256	15 360	57.750
3	0.375	0.75	48	384	23 040	86.625
4	0.500	1.00	64	512	30 720	115.500
5	0.625	1.25	80	640	38 400	144.375
6	0.750	1.50	96	768	46 080	173.250
7	0.875	1.75	112	896	53 760	202.125
8	1.000	2.00	128	1 024	61 440	231.000
9	1.125	2.25	144	1 152	69 120	259.875
10	1.250	2.50	160	1 280	76 800	288.750

OUNCE (LIQUID).

"One liquid or fluid ounce" is equal to:

0.007 812 5 liquid gallon   0.031 25 liquid quart

0.062 5 liquid pint   480 minims

0.25 gill   8 liquid dram

1.804 687 5 in^3 0.001 044 379 ft^3

2 tablespoons   32 liqud ounces = 1 liquid quart

16 liquid ounces = 1 liquid pint

8 liquid ounces = 1 cup   1/6 th liquid ounce =

1 teaspoon   128 liquid ounces = 1 liquid gallon

How to denote "liquid ounce" as "metric measures":

"One liquid ounce" is equal to:

0.029 572 7 liter   0.295 727 deciliter   29.572 70 ml
(obsolete, see pg.12)

How to denote "liquid or: fluid ounce(s)" as
"metric measures":

ounce(s) liquid	liter	deciliter (obsolete, see pq. 12)	milliliter
1	0.029 572 7	0.295 727	29.572 70
2	0.059 145 4	0.591 454	59.145 40
3	0.088 718 1	0.887 181	88.718 10
4	0.118 290 8	1.182 908	118.290 80
5	0.147 863 5	1.478 635	147.863 50
6	0.177 436 2	1.774 362	177.436 20
7	0.207 008 9	2.070 089	207.008 90
8	0.236 581 6	2.365 816	236.581 60
9	0.266 154 3	2.661 543	266.154 30
10	0.295 727 0	2.957 270	295.727 00

How to denote "liquid or: fluid ounce(s)" as other
"U.S. measures":

ounce(s) liquid	gallon liquid	quart liquid	pint liquid	gill liquid
1	0.007 812 5	0.031 25	0.062 5	0.25
2	0.015 625 0	0.062 50	0.125 0	0.50
3	0.023 437 5	0.093 75	0.187 5	0.75
4	0.031 250 0	0.125 00	0.250 0	1.00
5	0.039 062 5	0.156 25	0.312 5	1.25
6	0.046 875 0	0.187 50	0.375 0	1.50
7	0.054 687 5	0.218 75	0.437 5	1.75
8	0.062 500 0	0.250 00	0.500 0	2.00
9	0.070 312 5	0.281 25	0.562 5	2.25
10	0.078 125 0	0.312 50	0.625 0	2.50

How to denote "liquid or: fluid ounce(s)" as other
"U.S. measures":

ounce(s) liquid	dram liquid	minim liquid	in^3	ft^3
1	8	480	1.804 687 5	0.001 044 379
2	16	960	3.609 375 0	0.002 088 758
3	24	1 440	5.414 062 5	0.003 133 137
4	32	1 920	7.218 750 0	0.004 177 516
5	40	2 400	9.023 437 5	0.005 221 895
6	48	2 880	10.828 125 0	0.006 266 274
7	56	3 360	12.632 812 5	0.007 310 653
8	64	3 840	14.437 500 0	0.008 355 032
9	72	4 320	16.242 187 5	0.009 399 411
10	80	4 800	18.046 875 0	0.010 443 790

DRAM (LIQUID).

"One fluid or: liquid dram" is equal to:

   60 minims   0.125 liquid ounce   0.031 25 liquid gill

   0.007 812 5 liquid pint   0.003 906 25 liquid quart

   0.000 976 562 liquid gallon

   0.225 586 in^3 0.000 130 547 ft^3

How to denote "fluid or: liquid dram" as "metric measures":

"One fluid or: liquid dram" is equal to:

   0.003 696 588 liter   0.036 965 88 deciliter
      (obsolete, see page 12)
   3.696 588 milliliter

How to denote "liquid or: fluid dram(s)" as "metric measures":

dram(s) liquid	liter	deciliter (obsolete, see page 12)	milliliter
1	0.003 696 588	0.036 965 88	3.696 588
2	0.007 393 176	0.073 931 76	7.393 176
3	0.011 089 764	0.110 897 64	11.089 764
4	0.014 786 352	0.147 863 52	14.786 352
5	0.018 482 900	0.184 829 40	18.482 940
6	0.022 179 528	0.221 795 28	22.179 528
7	0.025 876 116	0.258 761 16	25.876 116
8	0.029 572 704	0.295 727 04	29.572 704
9	0.033 269 292	0.332 692 92	33.269 292
10	0.036 965 880	0.369 658 80	36.965 880

How to denote "liquid or: fluid dram(s)" as other "U.S. measures":

dram(s) liquid	minim liquid	ounce liquid	gill liquid	quart liquid	pint liquid
1	60	0.125	0.031 25	0.003 906 25	0.007 812 5
2	120	0.250	0.062 50	0.007 812 50	0.015 625 0
3	180	0.375	0.093 75	0.011 718 75	0.023 437 5
4	240	0.500	0.125 00	0.015 625 00	0.031 250 0
5	300	0.625	0.156 25	0.019 531 25	0.039 062 5
6	360	0.750	0.187 50	0.023 437 50	0.046 875 0
7	420	0.875	0.218 75	0.027 343 75	0.054 687 5
8	480	1.000	0.250 00	0.031 250 00	0.062 500 0
9	540	1.125	0.281 25	0.035 156 25	0.070 312 5
10	600	1.250	0.312 50	0.039 062 50	0.078 125 0

QUART (LIQUID).

"One liquid quart" is equal to:

    2 liquid pints   32 liquid ounces 57.75 in^3

    4 liquid quarts = 1 liquid gallon

How to denote "liquid quart" as "metric measures":

"One liquid quart" is equal to:

    0.946 326 4 liter   94.632 64 centiliter
                            (obsolete, <u>see</u> page 12)

    946.326 4 milliliter

How to denote "liquid quart(s)" as "metric measures":

quart(s) liquid	liter	milliliter
1	0.946 326 4	946.326 4
2	1.892 652 8	1 892.652 8
3	2.838 979 2	2 838.979 2
4	3.785 305 6	3 785.305 6
5	4.731 632 0	4 731.632 0
6	5.677 958 4	5 677.958 4
7	6.624 284 8	6 624.284 8
8	7.570 611 2	7 570.611 2
9	8.516 937 6	8 516.937 6
10	9.463 264 0	9 463.264 0

How to denote "liquid quart(s)" as other "U.S. measures":

quart(s) liquid	gallon liquid	pint liquid	gill liquid	ounce liquid	dram liquid	minim liquid
1	0.25	2	8	32	256	15 360
2	0.50	4	16	64	512	30 720
3	0.75	6	24	96	768	46 080
4	1.00	8	32	128	1 024	61 440
5	1.25	10	40	160	1 280	76 800
6	1.50	12	48	192	1 536	92 160
7	1.75	14	56	224	1 792	107 520
8	2.00	16	64	256	2 048	122 880
9	2.25	18	72	288	2 304	138 240
10	2.50	20	80	320	2 560	153 600

How to denote "liquid quart(s)" as other "U.S. measures":

quart(s) liquid	in^3	ft^3
1	57.75	0.033 420 14
2	115.50	0.066 840 28
3	173.25	0.100 260 42
4	231.00	0.133 680 56
5	288.75	0.167 100 70
6	346.50	0.200 520 84
7	404.25	0.233 940 98
8	462.00	0.267 361 12
9	519.75	0.300 781 26
10	577.50	0.334 201 40

GALLON (LIQUID).

"One liquid gallon" is equal to:

0.80 bushel	4 liquid quart	8 liquid pint
32 gill's	128 liquid ounces	
1 024 liquid drams		61 440 minim's
0.133 680 6 ft^3		231 in^3

How to denote "liquid gallon" as "metric measures":
"One liquid gallon" is equal to:

3.785 306 liter   3 785.306 milliliter

How to denote "liquid gallon(s)" as "metric measures":

gallon(s) liquid	liter	milliliter
1	3.785 306	3 785.306
2	7.570 612	7 570.612
3	11.355 918	11 355.918
4	15.141 224	15 141.224
5	18.926 530	18 926.530
6	22.711 836	22 711.836
7	26.497 142	26 497.142
8	30.282 448	30 282.448
9	34.067 754	34 067.754
10	37.853 060	37 853.060

How to denote "liquid gallon(s)" as other "U.S. measures":

gallon(s) liquid	quart liquid	pint liquid	gill liquid	ounce liquid	dram liquid	minim liquid
1	4	8	32	128	1 024	61 440
2	8	16	64	256	2 048	122 880
3	12	24	96	384	3 072	184 320
4	16	32	128	512	4 096	245 760
5	20	40	160	640	5 120	307 200
6	24	48	192	768	6 144	368 640
7	28	56	224	896	7 168	430 080
8	32	64	256	1 024	8 192	491 520
9	36	72	288	1 152	9 216	552 960
10	40	80	320	1 280	10 240	614 400

How to denote "liquid gallon(s)" as "U.S. cubic measures":

gallon(s) liquid	in^3	ft^3
1	231	0.133 680 6
2	462	0.267 361 2
3	693	0.401 841 8
4	924	0.534 722 4
5	1 155	0.668 403 0
6	1 386	0.802 083 6
7	1 617	0.935 764 2
8	1 848	1.069 444 8
9	2 079	1.203 125 4
10	2 310	1.336 806 0

BUSHEL.

"One bushel" is equal to:

4 dry pecks	32 dry quarts	63 dry pints
1.24 ft^3	2 150.42 in^3	

86 bushel's = 1 shaldron

How to denote "bushel" as "metric measures":

"One bushel" is equal to:

35.238 08 liter

3.523 808 dekaliter
(obsolete, see page 12)

0.352 380 8 hectoliter
(obsolete, see page 12)

How to denote "bushel(s)" as "metric measures":

bushel	liter	dekaliter	hectoliter	bushel per acre	hectoliter per acre
1	35.238 08	3.523 808	0.352 380 8	1	0.870 78
2	70.476 16	7.047 616	0.704 761 6	2	1.741 56
3	105.714 24	10.571 424	1.057 142 4	3	2.612 33
4	140.952 32	14.095 232	1.409 523 2	4	3.483 11
5	176.190 40	17.619 040	1.761 904 0	5	4.353 90
6	211.428 48	21.142 848	2.114 284 8	6	5.224 67
7	246.666 56	24.666 656	2.466 665 6	7	6.095 45
8	281.904 64	28.190 464	2.819 046 4	8	6.966 22
9	317.142 72	31.714 272	3.171 427 2	9	7.837 00
10	352.380 80	35.238 080	3.523 808 0	10	8.707 80

(o b s o l e t e , see p a g e 12)

DRACHEM (LIQUID).

"One fluid or: liquid drachem" is 3.696 7 "milliliters".

How to denote "liquid or: fluid drachem(s)" as "milliliter(s)":

drachem(s) liquid	milliliter(s)
1	3.696 7
2	7.393 4
3	11.090 1
4	14.786 9
5	18.483 6
6	22.180 3
7	25.877 0
8	29.573 7
9	33.270 4
10	36.967 2

MINIM (LIQUID).

"One fluid or: liquid minim" is equal to:

1 drop = 1/60 th liquid dram or: 0.016 666 7 liquid dram

60 minims = 1 liquid dram   0.002 083 33 liquid ounce

0.000 520 833 liquid gill   0.000 130 208 liquid pint

0.000 065 104 liquid quart   0.000 016 276 liquid gallon

0.003 760 in^3 0.000 002 176 ft^3

How to denote "liquid or: fluid minim" as "metric measures":

"One liquid or: fluid minim" is equal to:

0.000 061 610 liter   0.061 610 milliliter

How to denote "fluid or: liquid minim(s)" as"metric measures":

minim(s) liquid	milliliter(s)	deciliter(s) (obsolete, see page 127)	liter(s)
1	0.061 610	0.006 161 0	0.000 061 610
2	0.123 220	0.012 322 0	0.000 123 220
3	0.184 830	0.018 483 0	0.000 184 830
4	0.246 440	0.024 644 0	0.000 246 440
5	0.308 050	0.030 805 0	0.000 308 050
6	0.369 660	0.036 966 0	0.000 369 660
7	0.431 270	0.043 127 0	0.000 431 270
8	0.492 880	0.049 288 0	0.000 492 880
9	0.554 490	0.055 449 0	0.000 554 490
10	0.616 100	0.061 610 0	0.000 616 100

How to denote "fluid or: liquid minim(s)" as other "U.S. measures":

minim(s) liquid	gill liquid	dram liquid	ounce liquid	in^3
1	0.000 520 833	0.016 666 7	0.002 083 33	0.003 760
2	0.001 041 666	0.033 333 4	0.004 166 66	0.007 520
3	0.001 562 499	0.050 000 1	0.006 249 99	0.011 280
4	0.002 083 332	0.066 666 8	0.008 333 32	0.015 040
5	0.002 604 165	0.083 333 5	0.010 416 65	0.018 800
6	0.003 124 998	0.100 000 2	0.012 499 98	0.022 560
7	0.003 645 831	0.116 666 9	0.014 583 31	0.026 320
8	0.004 166 664	0.133 333 6	0.016 666 64	0.030 080
9	0.004 687 497	0.150 000 3	0.018 749 97	0.033 840
10	0.005 208 330	0.166 667 0	0.020 833 30	0.037 600

How to denote "liquid or: fluid dram(s)" as other
"U.S. measures":

dram(s) liquid	gallon liquid	in^3	ft^3
1	0.000 976 562	0.225 586	0.000 130 547
2	0.001 953 124	0.451 172	0.000 261 094
3	0.002 929 686	0.676 758	0.000 391 641
4	0.003 906 248	0.902 344	0.000 522 188
5	0.004 882 810	1.127 930	0.000 652 735
6	0.005 859 372	1.353 516	0.000 783 282
7	0.006 836 934	1.579 102	0.000 913 829
8	0.007 812 496	1.804 688	0.001 044 376
9	0.008 789 058	2.030 274	0.001 174 923
10	0.009 765 620	2.255 860	0.001 305 470

GILL (LIQUID).

"One gill fluid or: liquid" is equal to:

    1 920 minims   4 liquid ounces   32 liquid drams

    0.25 liquid pint   0.125 liquid quart

    0.031 25 liquid gallon   4 liquid gills = 1 liquid pint

    8 liquid gills = 1 liquid quart

    1 liquid gill = 7.218 75 in^3 or: 0.004 177 517 ft^3

How to denote "liquid gill" as "metric measures":

"One gill fluid or: liquid" is equal to:

    0.118 294 118 25 liter   1.182 941 182 5 deciliter (obsolete, see page 12)

    11.829 411 825 centiliter   118.294 118 25 milliliter
    (obsolete, see page 12)

How to denote "liquid or: fluid gill(s)" as "metric measures":

gill(s) liquid	liter	(obsolete, see pg.12 centiliter	milliliter
1	0.118 294 118 25	11.829 411 825	118.294 118 25
2	0.236 588 236 50	23.658 823 650	236.588 236 50
3	0.354 882 354 75	35.488 235 475	354.882 354 75
4	0.473 176 473 00	47.317 647 300	473.176 473 00
5	0.591 470 591 25	59.147 059 125	591.470 591 25
6	0.709 764 709 50	70.976 470 950	709.764 709 50
7	0.828 058 827 75	82.805 882 775	828.058 827 75
8	0.946 352 946 00	94.635 294 600	946.352 946 00
9	1.064 647 064 25	106.464 706 425	1 064.647 064 25
10	1.182 941 182 50	118.294 118 250	1 182.941 182 50

How to denote "liquid or: fluid gill(s)" as other "U.S. measures":

gill(s) liquid	minim liquid	dram liquid	ounce liquid	pint liquid	quart liquid	gallon liquid
1	1 920	32	4	0.25	0.125	0.031 25
2	3 840	64	8	0.50	0.250	0.062 50
3	5 760	96	12	0.75	0.375	0.093 75
4	7 680	128	16	1.00	0.500	0.125 00
5	9 600	160	20	1.25	0.625	0.156 25
6	11 520	192	24	1.50	0.750	0.187 50
7	13 440	224	28	1.75	0.875	0.218 75
8	15 360	256	32	2.00	1.000	0.250 00
9	17 280	288	36	2.25	1.125	0.281 25
10	19 200	320	40	2.50	1.250	0.312 50

How to denote "liquid or: fluid gill(s)" as other
"U.S. measures":

gill(s) liquid	in^3	ft^3
1	7.218 75	0.004 177 517
2	14.437 50	0.008 355 034
3	21.656 25	0.012 532 551
4	28.875 00	0.016 710 068
5	36.093 75	0.020 887 585
6	43.312 50	0.025 065 102
7	50.531 25	0.029 242 619
8	57.750 00	0.033 420 136
9	64.968 75	0.037 597 653
10	72.187 50	0.041 775 170

SCRUPLE (LIQUID).

"One fluid or: liquid scruple" is equal to: 1.232 2 milliliter.
How to denote "scruple(s)" as "milliliter(s)":

scruple(s) liquid	milliliter(s)
1	1.232 2
2	2.464 5
3	3.696 7
4	4.929 0
5	6.161 2
6	7.393 4
7	8.625 1
8	9.857 9
9	11.090 1
10	12.322 4

BARREL.

(A liquid, fluid and dry measure).

"One barrel" is equal to:

    $31\frac{1}{2}$ gallons   3.28 bushels

    2 barrels = 63 gallons = 1 hogshead

How to denote "barrel" as "metric measures":

"One barrel is equal to:

    158.988 liter

HOGSHEAD.

(A liquid measure of varying capacity).

"One hogshead" is equal to:

    63 gallons   8.42 ft^3

    2 barrels = 1 hogshead

"How to denote hogshead" as "metric measures":

"One hogshead" is equal to:

    317.976 liter

CUBIC INCH.

(As a liquid, fluid and various dry measures).

"One cubic inch" is equal to:

0.029 761 6 dry pint	0.014 880 8 dry quart
0.000 186 010 dry peck	0.000 465 025 dry bushel
265.974 liquid minims	4.432 900 liquid drams
0.554 112 6 liquid ounces	0.138 528 1 liquid gill
0.034 632 03 liquid pint	0.017 316 02 liquid quart
0.004 320 004 liquid gallon	

$57.75 \text{ in}^3 = 1$ liquid quart (2 liquid pints)

$67.200\ 6 \text{ in}^3 = 1$ dry quart (2 dry pints)

$231 \text{ in}^3 = 1$ liquid gallon (4 liquid quarts = 8 liquid pints)

$537.605 \text{ in}^3 = 1$ dry peck (8 dry quarts = 16 dry pints)

$2\ 150.42 \text{ in}^3 = 1$ dry bushel (4 dry pecks = 32 dry quarts)

How to denote "cubic inch" as "metric liquid or: fluid measures":

"One cubic inch" is equal to:

16 387.064 milliliters	(obsolete, see page 12) 16.387 064 centiliters
0.001 639 deciliter (obsolete, see page 12)	0.016 387 liter

How to denote "cubic inch(es)" as "metric liquid measures":

in^3	milliliter	(obsolete, see page 12) centiliter	deciliter	liter
1	16 387.064	16.387 064	0.001 639	0.016 387
2	32 774.128	32.774 128	0.003 278	0.032 774
3	49 161.192	49.161 192	0.004 917	0.049 161
4	65 548.256	65.548 256	0.006 556	0.065 548
5	81 935.320	81.935 320	0.008 195	0.081 935
6	98 322.384	98.322 384	0.009 834	0.098 322
7	114 709.448	114.709 448	0.011 473	0.114 709
8	131 096.512	131.096 512	0.013 112	0.131 096
9	147 483.576	147.483 576	0.014 751	0.147 483
10	163 870.640	163.870 640	0.016 390	0.163 870

How to denote "cubic inch(es)" as other "U.S. liquid and dry measures":

in^3	minim liquid	dram liquid	ounce liquid	gill liquid
1	265.974	4.432 90	0.554 112 6	0.138 528 1
2	531.948	8.865 80	1.108 225 2	0.277 056 2
3	797.922	13.298 70	1.662 337 8	0.415 584 3
4	1 063.896	17.731 60	2.216 450 4	0.554 112 4
5	1 329.870	22.164 50	2.770 563 0	0.692 640 5
6	1 595.844	26.597 40	3.324 675 6	0.831 168 6
7	1 861.818	31.030 30	3.878 788 2	0.969 696 7
8	2 127.792	35.463 20	4.432 900 8	1.108 224 8
9	2 393.766	39.896 10	4.987 013 4	1.246 752 9
10	2 659.740	44.329 00	5.541 126 0	1.385 281 0

How to denote "cubic inch(es)" as other "U.S. liquid and dry measures":

in^3	pint liquid	pint dry	quart dry	peck dry	bushel dry
1	0.034 632 03	0.029 762	0.014 881	0.001 86	0.000 465
2	0.069 264 06	0.059 524	0.029 762	0.003 72	0.000 930
3	0.103 896 09	0.089 286	0.044 643	0.005 58	0.001 395
4	0.138 528 12	0.119 048	0.059 524	0.007 44	0.001 860
5	0.173 160 15	0.148 810	0.074 405	0.009 30	0.002 325
6	0.207 792 18	0.178 572	0.089 286	0.011 16	0.002 790
7	0.242 424 21	0.208 334	0.104 167	0.013 02	0.003 255
8	0.277 056 24	0.238 096	0.119 048	0.014 88	0.003 720
9	0.311 688 27	0.267 858	0.133 929	0.016 74	0.004 185
10	0.346 320 30	0.297 620	0.148 810	0.018 60	0.004 650

CUBIC FOOT (FEET).

(As "fluid or: liquid measures").

"One cubic foot" is equal to:

459 603 liquid minims	7 660.052 liquid drams
957.506 5 liquid ounces	239.376 6 liquid gills
29.922 08 liquid quarts	7.480 519 liquid gallons

$0.016\ 710\ 07\ ft^3 = 1$ liquid pint

$0.033\ 420\ 14\ ft^3 = 1$ liquid quart

How to denote "cubic foot" as "metric liquid measures":

"One cubic foot" is equal to:

28.316 05 liters	283.160 5 deciliters (obsolete, see page 12)
2 831.605 centiliters (obsolete, see page 12)	28 316.05 milliliters

How to denote "cobic foot; feet" as "metric liquid measures":

ft^3	milli liters	(obsolete, see page 12) centiliters	deciliters	liters
1	28 316.05	2 831.605	283.160 5	28.316 05
2	56 632.10	5 663.210	566.321 0	56.632 10
3	84 948.15	8 494.815	849.481 5	84.948 15
4	113 264.20	11 326.420	1 132.642 0	113.264 20
5	141 580.25	14 158.025	1 415.802 5	141.580 25
6	169 896.30	16 989.630	1 698.963 0	169.896 30
7	198 212.35	19 821.235	1 982.123 5	198.212 35
8	226 528.40	22 652.840	2 265.284 0	226.528 40
9	254 844.45	25 484.445	2 548.444 5	254.844 45
10	283 160.50	28 316.050	2 831.605 0	283.160 50

How to denote "cubic foot; feet" as other "U.S. measures":

ft^3	gallon liquid	quart liquid	pint liquid	ounce liquid
1	7.480 519	29.922 08	59.844 16	957.506 5
2	14.961 038	59.844 16	119.688 32	1 915.013 0
3	22.441 557	89.766 24	179.532 48	2 872.519 5
4	29.922 076	119.688 32	239.376 64	3 830.026 0
5	37.402 595	149.610 40	299.220 80	4 787.532 5
6	44.883 114	179.532 48	359.064 96	5 745.039 0
7	52.363 633	209.454 56	418.909 12	6 702.545 5
8	59.844 152	239.376 64	478.753 28	7 660.052 0
9	67.324 671	269.298 72	538.597 44	8 617.558 5
10	74.805 190	299.220 80	598.441 60	9 575.065 0

How to denote "cubic foot; feet" as other "U.S. measures":

ft^3	gill liquid	dram liquid	minim liquid	in^3
1	239.376 6	7 660.052	459 603.1	1 728
2	478.753 2	15 320.104	919 206.2	3 456
3	718.129 8	22 980.156	1 378 809.3	5 184
4	957.506 4	30 640.208	1 838 412.4	6 912
5	1 196.883 0	38 300.260	2 298 015.5	8 640
6	1 436.259 6	45 960.312	2 757 618.6	10 368
7	1 675.636 2	53 620.364	3 217 221.7	12 096
8	1 915.012 8	61 280.416	3 676 824.8	13 824
9	2 154.389 4	68 940.468	4 136 427.9	15 552
10	2 393.766 0	76 600.520	4 596 031.0	17 280

THE MEASURE(S) OF TEMPERATURE(S).

Four types of "thermometer" are most commonly used to measure "temperature".

Celsius scale. (Celsius, degree). Symbol: ^{o}C
Formerly called the "centigrade scale".
A temperature scale in which the freezing point of water at normal atmospheric pressure is 0 ^{o}C and the boiling point is 100 ^{o}C
"One degree Celsius equals one Kelvin, exactly.

Fahrenheit scale. (Fahrenheit, degree). Symbol: ^{o}F
A temperature scale in which "zero" is the temperature of a mixture of equal weights of snow and common salt.
On this scale, the freezing point of water is +32 ^{o}F and the boiling point is +212 ^{o}F, under standard atmospheric pressure.

Kelvin scale: Thermodynamic temperature. (Kelvin, degree).
Symbol: K
The absolute scale of temperature, based on the average Kinetic energy per molecule of a perfect gas.
"Zero" is equal to -273 ^{o}Celsius or -459.4 ^{o}Fahrenheit.

Reaumur scale. (Reaumur, degree). Symbol: ^{o}R
The thermometric scale in which the "zero" point corresponds to the temperature of melting ice, and 80 ^{o}R to the temperature of boiling water.

FORMULAS.

The following formulas may be used to convert temperature readings taken on one scale into their equivalents on any of the other scales.

(Degrees Celsius x 9/5) plus 32 = degrees Fahrenheit.

Degrees Celsius x 4/5 = degrees Reaumur.

(Degrees Fahrenheit minus 32) x 5/9 = degrees Celsius.

(Degrees Fahrenheit minus 32) x 4/9 = degrees Reaumur.

Degrees Reaumur x 5/4 = degrees Celsius.

(Degrees Reaumur x 9/4) plus 32 = degrees Fahrenheit.

THE "CLINICAL THERMOMETER" which is used by physicians and hospitals to read body temperature.
Normal average BODY TEMPERATURE is 98.6 °F = 37 °C
BODY TEMPERATURE may fluctuate between 97 °F = 36.1 °C
to 99 °F = 37.2 °C and still be considered as being normal.

TEMPERATURE.

Above +0 °C denoted as above +32 °F

The denoted temperatures are from 0 °C freezing point of water to the 100 °C boiling point of water.

+°C = +°F	+°C = +°F	+°C = +°F	+°C = +°F	+°C = +°F
0 = 32	21 = 69.8	42 = 107.6	63 = 145.4	84 = 183.2
1 = 33.8	22 = 71.6	43 = 109.4	64 = 147.2	85 = 185
2 = 35.6	23 = 73.4	44 = 111.2	65 = 149	86 = 186.8
3 = 37.4	24 = 75.2	45 = 113	66 = 150.8	87 = 188.6
4 = 39.2	25 = 77	46 = 114.8	67 = 152.6	88 = 190.4
5 = 41	26 = 78.8	47 = 116.6	68 = 154.4	89 = 192.2
6 = 42.8	27 = 80.6	48 = 118.4	69 = 156.2	90 = 194
7 = 44.6	28 = 82.4	49 = 120.2	70 = 158	91 = 195.8
8 = 46.4	29 = 84.2	50 = 122	71 = 159.8	92 = 197.6
9 = 48.2	30 = 86	51 = 123.8	72 = 161.6	93 = 199.4
10 = 50	31 = 87.8	52 = 125.6	73 = 163.4	94 = 201.2
11 = 51.8	32 = 89.6	53 = 127.4	74 = 165.2	95 = 203
12 = 53.6	33 = 91.4	54 = 129.2	75 = 167	96 = 204.8
13 = 55.4	34 = 93.2	55 = 131	76 = 168.8	97 = 206.6
14 = 57.2	35 = 95	56 = 132.8	77 = 170.6	98 = 208.4
15 = 59	36 = 96.8	57 = 134.6	78 = 172.4	99 = 210.2
16 = 60.8	37 = 98.6	58 = 136.4	79 = 174.2	100 = 212
17 = 62.6	38 = 100.4	59 = 138.2	80 = 176	
18 = 64.4	39 = 102.2	60 = 140	81 = 177.8	
19 = 66.2	40 = 104	61 = 141.8	82 = 179.6	
20 = 68	41 = 105.8	62 = 143.6	83 = 181.4	

TEMPERATURE.

Above +32 °F denoted as above +0 °C

The denoted temperatures are from +32 °F freezing point of water to the +212 °F boiling point of water.

+ °F =	+ °C	+ °F =	+ °C	+ °F =	+ °C	+ °F =	+ °C
32 =	0	53 =	11.67	74 =	23.33	95 =	35
33 =	0.56	54 =	12.22	75 =	23.89	96 =	35.56
34 =	1.11	55 =	12.78	76 =	24.44	97 =	36.11
35 =	1.67	56 =	13.33	77 =	25	98 =	36.67
36 =	2.22	57 =	13.89	78 =	25.56	99 =	37.22
37 =	2.78	58 =	14.44	79 =	26.11	100 =	37.78
38 =	3.33	59 =	15	80 =	26.67	101 =	38.33
39 =	3.89	60 =	15.56	81 =	27.22	102 =	38.89
40 =	4.44	61 =	16.11	82 =	27.78	103 =	39.44
41 =	5	62 =	16.67	83 =	28.33	104 =	40
42 =	5.56	63 =	17.22	84 =	28.89	105 =	40.56
43 =	6.11	64 =	17.78	85 =	29.44	106 =	41.11
44 =	6.67	65 =	18.33	86 =	30	107 =	41.67
45 =	7.22	66 =	18.89	87 =	30.56	108 =	42.22
46 =	7.78	67 =	19.44	88 =	31.11	109 =	42.78
47 =	8.33	68 =	20	89 =	31.67	110 =	43.33
48 =	8.89	69 =	20.56	90 =	32.22	111 =	43.89
49 =	9.44	70 =	21.11	91 =	32.78	112 =	44.44
50 =	10	71 =	21.67	92 =	33.33	113 =	45
51 =	10.56	72 =	22.22	93 =	33.89	114 =	45.56
52 =	11.11	73 =	22.78	94 =	34.44	115 =	46.11

+ °F =	+°C	+ °F =	+°C	+ °F =	+°C	+ °F =	+°C
116 =	46.67	140 =	60	164 =	73.33	188 =	86.67
117 =	47.22	141 =	60.56	165 =	73.89	189 =	87.22
118 =	47.78	142 =	61.11	166 =	74.44	190 =	87.78
119 =	48.33	143 =	61.67	167 =	75	191 =	88.33
120 =	48.89	144 =	62.22	168 =	75.56	192 =	88.89
121 =	49.44	145 =	62.78	169 =	76.11	193 =	89.44
122 =	50	146 =	63.33	170 =	76.67	194 =	90
123 =	50.56	147 =	63.89	171 =	77.22	195 =	90.56
124 =	51.11	148 =	64.44	172 =	77.78	196 =	91.11
125 =	51.67	149 =	65	173 =	78.33	197 =	91.67
126 =	52.22	150 =	65.56	174 =	78.89	198 =	92.22
127 =	52.78	151 =	66.11	175 =	79.44	199 =	92.78
128 =	53.33	152 =	66.67	176 =	80	200 =	93.33
129 =	53.89	153 =	67.22	177 =	80.56	201 =	93.89
130 =	54.44	154 =	67.78	178 =	81.11	202 =	94.44
131 =	55	155 =	68.33	179 =	81.67	203 =	95
132 =	55.56	156 =	68.89	180 =	82.22	204 =	95.56
133 =	56.11	157 =	69.44	181 =	82.78	205 =	96.11
134 =	56.67	158 =	70	182 =	83.33	206 =	96.67
135 =	57.22	159 =	70.56	183 =	83.89	207 =	97.22
136 =	57.78	160 =	71.11	184 =	84.44	208 =	97.78
137 =	58.33	161 =	71.67	185 =	85	209 =	98.33
138 =	58.89	162 =	72.22	186 =	85.56	210 =	98.89
139 =	59.44	163 =	72.78	187 =	86.11	211 =	99.44
						212 =	100

TEMPERATURE.

Below -0 Celsius degrees freezing point denoted as:

below the +32 Fahrenheit degrees freezing point.

-°C	=	°F	-°C	=	°F	-°C	=	°F	-°C	=	°F	-°C	=	°F
0	=	+32	22	=	-7.6	44	=	-47.2	66	=	-86.8	88	=	-126.4
1	=	+30.2	23	=	-9.4	45	=	-49	67	=	-88.6	89	=	-128.2
2	=	+28 4	24	=	-11.2	46	=	-50.8	68	=	-90.4	90	=	-130
3	=	+26.6	25	=	-13	47	=	-52.6	69	=	-92.2	91	=	-131.8
4	=	+24.8	26	=	-14.8	48	=	-54.4	70	=	-94	92	=	-133.6
5	=	+23	27	=	-16.6	49	=	-56.2	71	=	-95.8	93	=	-135.4
6	=	+21.2	28	=	-18.4	50	=	-58	72	=	-97.6	94	=	-137.2
7	=	+19.4	29	=	-20.2	51	=	-59.8	73	=	-99.4	95	=	-139
8	=	+17.6	30	=	-22	52	=	-61.6	74	=	-101.2	96	=	-140.8
9	=	+15.8	31	=	-23.8	53	=	-63.4	75	=	-103	97	=	-142.6
10	=	+14	32	=	-25.6	54	=	-65.2	76	=	-104.8	98	=	-144.4
11	=	+12.2	33	=	-27.4	55	=	-67	77	=	-106.6	99	=	-146.2
12	=	+10.4	34	=	-29.2	56	=	-68.8	78	=	-108.4	100	=	-148
13	=	+ 8.6	35	=	-31	57	=	-70.6	79	=	-110.2			
14	=	+6.8	36	=	-32.8	58	=	-72.4	80	=	-112			
15	=	+5	37	=	-34.6	59	=	-74.2	81	=	-113.8			
16	=	+3.2	38	=	-36.4	60	=	-76	82	=	-115.6			
17	=	+1.4	39	=	-38.2	61	=	-77.8	83	=	-117.4			
18	=	-0.6	40	=	-40	62	=	-79.6	84	=	-119.2			
19	=	-2.2	41	=	-41.8	63	=	-81.4	85	=	-121			
20	=	-4	42	=	-43.6	64	=	-83.2	86	=	-122.8			
21	=	-5.8	43	=	-45.4	65	=	-85	87	=	-124.6			

TEMPERATURE.

Below the +32 Fahrenheit degrees freezing point denoted as:

below the -0 Celsius degrees freezing point.

+ °F	=	- °C	± °F	=	- °C	- °F	=	- °C	- °F	=	- °C
+32	=	0	+10	=	12.2	-12	=	24.49	-34	=	36.81
+31	=	0.5	+9	=	12.7	-13	=	25.05	-35	=	37.37
+30	=	1.1	+8	=	13.3	-14	=	25.61	-36	=	37.93
+29	=	1.6	+7	=	13.8	-15	=	26.17	-37	=	38.49
+28	=	2.2	+6	=	14.4	-16	=	26.73	-38	=	39.05
+27	=	2.7	+5	=	15	-17	=	27.29	-39	=	39.61
+26	=	3.3	+4	=	15.5	-18	=	27.85	-40	=	40.17
+25	=	3.9	+3	=	16.1	-19	=	28.41	-41	=	40.73
+24	=	4.4	+2	=	16.6	-20	=	28.97	-42	=	41.33
+23	=	5	+1	=	17.2	-21	=	29.53	-43	=	41.89
+22	=	5.5	±0	=	17.77	-22	=	30.09	-44	=	42.45
+21	=	6.1	-1	=	18.33	-23	=	30.65	-45	=	43.01
+20	=	6.6	-2	=	18.89	-24	=	31.21	-46	=	43.57
+19	=	7.2	-3	=	19.45	-25	=	31.77	-47	=	44.13
+18	=	7.7	-4	=	20.01	-26	=	32.33	-48	=	44.69
+17	=	8.3	-5	=	20.57	-27	=	32.89	-49	=	45.25
+16	=	8.8	-6	=	21.13	-28	=	33.45	-50	=	45.81
+15	=	9.4	-7	=	21.69	-29	=	34.01	-51	=	46.37
+14	=	10	-8	=	22.25	-30	=	34.57	-52	=	46.93
+13	=	10.5	-9	=	22.81	-31	=	35.13	-53	=	47.49
+12	=	11.1	-10	=	23.37	-32	=	35.69	-54	=	48.05
+11	=	11.6	-11	=	23.93	-33	=	36.25	-55	=	48.61

- °F	=	- °C	- °F	=	- °C
-56	=	49.17	-81	=	63.17
-57	=	49.73	-82	=	63.73
-58	=	50.29	-83	=	64.29
-59	=	50.85	-84	=	64.85
-60	=	51.41	-85	=	65.41
-61	=	51.97	-86	=	65.97
-62	=	52.53	-87	=	66.53
-63	=	53.09	-88	=	67.09
-64	=	53.65	-89	=	67.65
-65	=	54.21	-90	=	68.21
-66	=	54.77	-91	=	68.77
-67	=	55.33	-92	=	69.33
-68	=	55.89	-93	=	69.89
-69	=	56.45	-94	=	70.45
-70	=	57.01	-95	=	71.01
-71	=	57.57	-96	=	71.57
-72	=	58.13	-97	=	72.13
-73	=	58.69	-98	=	72.69
-74	=	59.25	-99	=	73.25
-75	=	59.81	-100	=	73.81
-76	=	60.37			
-77	=	60.93			
-78	=	61.49			
-79	=	62.05			
-80	=	62.61			

MILLIBAR. (obsolete).

A unit of atmospheric pressure equal to one thousandth of a bar.

BAR. (obsolete).

The cgs international unit of pressure, equal to 1 000 000 dynes a square centimeter or a pressure of 29.531 inches of mercury at 32 °F

MILLIBAR and BAR is obsolete;
==============================
a poor choice of pressure
=============================
units. See page 12.
===================

The cgs system is obsolete,
=============================

use instead:

"pascal" the metric unit of pressure.

"kilopascals"

1 000 pascals·atmospheric pressure is approximately 100 kilopascals.

MEASURE OF TIME.

"Time" is measured, and computed in the "metric system" with
the same values as in the "U.S. system".
The "unit" is the "second".
    "One second" is defined as the duration of:
    9 192 631 770 cycles of the radiation associated with
    a specified transition of the ground state of the
    cesium-133 atom.
All small and large portions of time are "time spane(s)",
"spane(s) of time", or "periode(s) of time".
Day(s), month(s), season(s), etc. are technical, mechanical,
or industrial measured "periode(s) of time".

MEASURE OF VELOCITY.

"Velocity" denotes the moving speed of a certain kind of a
particular object in a specified, measured distance and
spane of time.
Dividing distance by time gives speed.
The "unit" for speed is the "meter per second" (m/s).
"Velocity" as "metric values".
    1 km/h = 0.277 8 m/s
    1 m/s = 3.6 km/h

"metric measurements" denoted as "U.S. measurements":

$$1 \text{ m/s} = 3.281 \text{ ft/s}$$
$$1 \text{ m/s} = 196.9 \text{ ft/min}$$
$$1 \text{ m/s} = 2.237 \text{ M/h}$$

"U.S. measurements" denoted as "metric measurements":

$$1 \text{ ft/s} = 0.303 \text{ 8 m/s}$$
$$1 \text{ ft/min} = 0.005 \text{ 08 m/s}$$
$$1 \text{ M/h} = 0.447 \text{ 0 m/s}$$

MEASURE OF ACCELERATION.

"Acceleration" denotes a rate gain of velocity, of "metric acceleration" of standard gravity:

$$9.806 \text{ m/s}^2$$
$$980.6 \text{ cm/s}^2$$

"U.S. acceleration" of standard gravity:

$$32.2 \text{ ft/s}^2$$

"U.S. measurements" denoted as "metric measurements":

$$1 \text{ ft/s}^2 = 0.304 \text{ 8 m/s}^2$$

MEASURE OF FORCE.

"Metric unit" is: Newton

The "newton" is the force that will give weight of one kilogram an acceleration of one meter per second squared. On the earth gravity exerts a force of approximately 9.8 newtons on a weight of one kilogram.

MEASUREMENT OF "WORK".

"metric":

Joule is the unit. It is the work done by a force of one newton over a distance of one meter.

MEASURE OF "POWER".

"metric":

Watt is the unit of power. It is the rate of doing work. Power the rate of one Joule per second is one watt.

Watt.

"One watt" = 100/981 of one kilogrammeter. (obsolete; <u>see</u> page 12).

SPEED.
"rounded off".

Statute Mile(s) per hour

denoted as:

Kilometer(s) per hour

Kilometer(s) per hour

denoted as:

Statute Mile(s) per hour

M/h	km/h
5	8
10	16
15	24
20	32
25	40
30	48
35	56
40	64
45	72
50	80
55	88
60	96
65	104
70	112
75	120
80	128
85	136
90	144
95	152
100	160

km/h	M/h
5	3
10	6
15	9
20	12
25	15
30	18
35	21
40	24
45	27
50	30
55	33
60	36
65	39
70	42
75	45
80	48
85	51
90	54
95	57
100	60

Autotire pressure: 30 lbs/sq. in = 2.109 kg/cm^2

COMMON HOUSEHOLD MEASURES AND WEIGHTS.

"U.S. measures" denoted as "metric measures":

1 teaspoon = 5 ml = 0.005 liter

1 tablespoon = 15 ml = 0.015 liter

½ cup = 59 ml = 0.059 liter

1 cup = 118 ml = 0.118 liter

12 units = 1 dozen   20 units = 1 score

12 dozen = 1 gross   12 gross (144 units) = 1 gr.gross

COMMON CLOTHING SIZES.

metric	U.S.		metric	U.S.
MEN			**WOMEN**	
shoes			**shoes**	
38	6		34	4
39	6½		35	5
40	7		36	6
41	8		37	6½
42	8½		38	7
43	9		38½	8
44	10		**dress**	
45	11		38	10
shirt			40	12
36	14		42	14
37	14½		44	16
38	15			
39	15¼			
40	15½			
41	16			

NOTE:
The above sizes are "French metric sizes"
(generally)- not the same elswhere.
For example: A dress size 38 in France is:
a dress size 40 in Germany
a dress size 42 in Italy
a dress size 30 in Spain
a dress size 36 in Switzerland

RULES FOR COMPUTING.

Area of rectangular = length x widths.

Capacity of cubic = length x widths x depth.

Capacity of cylinder = 0.785 4 x (diameter)^2 x height.

Capacity of a unit with tapered sides = vertical height
x $\frac{1}{2}$ sum of top and
bottom area.

Circumference of circle = diameter x 3.14 .

Area of circle = 0.785 x diameter x diameter.

<u>For</u> Common Equivalents and Conversions see page 154 - 155

ABBREVIATIONS IN ALPHABETICAL SEQUENCE.

A	acre	acre	acre inch	acre in
	acre foot	acre ft	are	a
	ampere	A	assay ton	assay t

B	barrel	bbl	building	bdg
	bushel	bsh	board foot; feet	bd ft

C	cable's length	c l	candela	cd
	carat	c	celsius, degree	$^{\circ}$C
	centare	ca	centigram	cg
	centiliter	cl	centimeter	cm
	centi stere	c stere	chain	ch
	cord	cd	cubic centimeter	cm^3
	cubic decimeter	dm^3	cubic dekameter	dam^3
	cubic foot	ft^3	cubic hectometer	hm^3
	cubic inch	in^3	cubic kilometer	km^3
	cubic meter	m^3	cubic yard	yd^3

D	decigram	dg	deciliter	dl
	decimeter	dm	degree	
	dekagram	dag	dekaliter	dal
	dekameter	dam	drachem	drachem
	dram, avoir-dupois	dr avdp	dram, troy	dr tr

F	fathom	fath	foot; feet	ft
	furlong	furlong		

G	gallon	gal	gill	gill
	grain	grain	gram	g
	gross Hundred-weight	gr cwt	short Hundred-weight	cwt

H	hand	hand	hectare	ha
	hectogram	hg	hectoliter	hl
	hectometer	hm	hecto stere	h stere
	hogshead	hhd	horsepower	hp
	hundredweight	cwt		

I	inch	in	International Nautical Mile	INM

K	keg	keg	Kelvin, degree	K
	kilogram	kg	kilometer	km
	kilowatt	kW	knot	knot

L	link	link	liquid	liq
	liter	l		

M	meter	m	mile	mi
	milligram	mg	milliliter	ml
	millimeter	mm	minim	minim

O	ounce	oz	ounce, avoirdu-pois	oz avdp
	ounce, liquid	liq oz	ounce, troy	oz tr

P	peck	peck	pennyweight	dwt
	pole	pole	pint, liquid	liq pt
	pound	lb	pound, avoirdu-pois	lb avdp
	pound, troy	lb tr	pascal	pa

Qu	quart	qt	quart, liquid	liq qt

R	Reaumur, degree	R	rod	rod

S	scruple	scr	second	s
	square centimeter	cm^2	square decimeter	dm^2
	square dekameter	dam^2	square foot; feet	ft^2
	square inch	in^2	square hectometer	hm^2
	square meter	m^2	square kilometer	km^2
	square mile	mi^2	square millimeter	mm^2
	square yard	yd^2	stere	stere

T	ton, long	long ton	ton, metric	t
	ton, short	short ton		
Y	yard	yd		

I N D E X

- 148 -

League (land) page 32

Cable's length page 33

Equador grad page 33

MEASURES OF SURFACES.   Page 34 - 50

Explanations page 34

MEASURES OF TEMPERATURES.   Page 129 - 136

T H E   E N D

- N O T E S -

Approximate Common Equivalents.   "rounded off"

1 inch	= 25 millimeters
1 foot	= 0.3 meter
1 yard	= 0.9 meter
1 mile	= 1.6 kilometers
1 square inch	= 6.5 square centimeters
1 square foot	= 0.09 square meter
1 square yard	= 0.8 square meter
1 acre	= 0.4 hectare
1 cubic inch	= 16 cubic centimeters
1 cubic foot	= 0.03 cubic meter
1 cubic yard	= 0.8 cubic meter
1 quart (1qU)	= 1 liter
1 gallon	= 0.004 cubic meter
1 ounce (avdp)	= 28 grams
1 pound (avdp)	= 0.45 kilogram
1 horsepower	= 0.75 kilowatt
1 millimeter	= 0.04 inch
1 meter	= 3.3 feet
1 meter	= 1.1 yards
1 kilometer	= 0.6 mile
1 squ. centimeter	= 0.16 square inch
1 square meter	= 1.2 square yards
1 hectare	= 2.5 acres
1 cubic centimeter	= 0.06 cubic inch
1 cubic meter	= 35 cubic feet
1 cubic meter	= 1.3 cubic yards
1 liter	= 1 quart (liquid)
1 cubic meter	= 260 gallons
1 gram	= 0.035 ounces (avdp)
1 kilowatt	= 1.3 horsepower

Conversions Accurate to Parts Per Million.

inches x 25.4	= millimeters (exact)
feet x 0.3048	= meters (exact)
yards x 0.9144	= meters (exact)
miles x 1.609 34	= kilometers
square inches x 6.4516	= square centimeters (exact)
square feet x 0.092 903 0	= square meters
square yards x 0.836 127	= square meters
acres x 0.404 686	= hectares
cubic inches x 16.3871	= cubic centimeters
cubic feet x 0.028 316 8	= cubic meters
cubic yards x 0.764 555	= cubic meters
quarts (1qu) x 0.946 353	= liters
gallons x 0.003 785 41	= cubic meters

- N O T E S -

ounces (avdp) x 28.3495	= grams
pounds (avdp) x 0.453 592	= kilograms
horsepower x 0.745 700	= kilowatts
millimeters x 0.039 370 1	= inches
meters x 3.280 84	= feet
meters x 1.093 61	= yards
kilometers x 0.621 371	= miles
squ. centimeters x 0.155 000	= square inches
square meters x 10.7639	= square feet
square meters x 1.195 99	= square yards
hectares x 2.471 85	= acres
cu. centimeters x 0.061 023 7	= cubic inches
cubic meters x 35.3147	= cubic feet
cubic meters x 1.307 95	= cubic yards
liters x 1.056 69	= quarts (liquid)
cubic meters x 264.172	= gallons
grams x 0.035 274 0	= ounces (avdp)
kilograms x 2.204 62	= pounds (avdp)
kilowatts x 1.341 02	= horsepower